Rigger

Nancy

Keep those dogs

Busied!

Rigger

From High School to High Steel

Larry James Neff

Blue Heron Book Works

ISBN 13: 978-0-692-28703-3
ISBN 10: 0692287035

Blue Heron Books Works
www.blueheronbookworks.com

Printed by CreateSpace, an Amazon.com Company

DEDICATION

This book is dedicated to my union brothers and sisters, the members of the United Steelworkers of America. In particular, it is for all those who have died in accidents within the industry. They will not be forgotten as long as there is someone to tell their stories.

CONTENTS

ACKNOWLEDGEMENTS

My heartfelt thanks goes to my editor and publisher Bathsheba Monk for her knowledge and assistance in producing this book.

My respect and love to my partner Jane Gill for her belief in and support for my fantasy of writing a book.

"Shop Talk" was previously published in The Manuscript 2012-2013. Bethlehem, PA: Moravian College, 2013. Portions of "Freihoffer's Bakery" were previously published in The Manuscript 2013-2014. Bethlehem, PA: Moravian College, 2014. My sincere thanks to the editors, especially Katie Makoski, as well as to Dr. Joyce Hinnefeld, Faculty Advisor, for their aid in helping me publish these stories. It was greatly appreciated.

INTRODUCTION

In the spring of 2012 I sat down and put pen to paper (literally, because I can't type), beginning this book. I had intended it to be a light-hearted collection of stories about the jobs I had pursued during my life. I have told these stories to family and friends many times, usually evoking smiles and laughs. As I began writing, I related my stories in this fashion.

But as I went along, my writing underwent a deeper and more profound change. The stories evolved into an exercise in duality: survival. My every day, personal survival in a very dangerous industry, and the survival of that industry in an ever-changing and hostile corporate world.

The stories within my book are true. They are based on my best recollection of events that transpired many years ago. I am particularly taking advantage of the fact that, at my age, my long-term memory is quite vivid even though I can't always remember what I did yesterday. I have changed some names of individuals or places, out of respect or to maintain anonymity.

1 BETHLEHEM STEEL PREP

I am looking back to an era in "Steel Town" Bethlehem PA that most of us over the age of fifty remember. It was an era without video games, cell phones, computers, WIFI, texting. An era when workers were scarce and jobs were plentiful. An era when your parents knew you did something wrong even before you got home, not because they got a text, but because your phone was on a party line. It was an age of innocence. You played mock war games in the tall field grass with friends like Frankie, Stevie, and Rocky. You played touch football or whiffle ball in the street, and watched in awe when the firecrackers that you lit exploded. You rode bicycles that were heavier than your fathers' new Corvair. You stood in line waiting to be picked for a basketball game with the older guys. You played hide and seek until the wee hour of 9 PM. It was a time when you were convinced that the old woman next door was a witch, only to find out she was a Hungarian émigré who had come here after the Eastern European revolt in 1956, and was a walking repository for home remedies and natural cures and the best baker of apple strudel west of Budapest.

If you grew up on the North or South Side, you were lulled to sleep by the rhythmic thumping of the drop forge hammers. You would hear the constant chugging of the PB&NE engines bumping cars or hauling submarine cars carrying three hundred tons of molten iron. If you lived on the East Side, you would lay in bed and hear the buzzing of the hot and cold saws in the shipping yards. Back then, December trips to Third Street to Christmas shop or see the lights meant you passed the blast furnaces with their ethereal glowing lights from iron being tapped, and their tulip-like burner stacks belching ignited methane blue gas. Usually your parents took the opportunity to explain to you that this was the entrance to Hell. You listened in awe and behaved like an angel. At least until after Christmas. An entrance to Hell wasn't far from the truth as I saw many years later while working there. It may not have been the gates of hell, but it certainly was the embarkation point to eternity for many workers who entered the plant and never got to go home to their families.

It was a grand age for nepotism. If your father worked at Bethlehem Steel, you would inevitably follow him. Being saddled with homework every night, I admired the fact that my father would go to work, put his eight hours in, and come home. After that it was all free time…..no homework. The local steel unions had even negotiated that your lunch time was included in your eight-hour shift. So I suppose I was mentally grooming myself for a future as a steelworker.

As a senior in high school, the thoughts about my future began after the safety net of twelve years of public schools. The free ride was over. I had endured the years on a higher than normal IQ and a gift for being the class clown. I excelled in history, reading, writing, languages, and had a love of art. By my sophomore year I could sketch Snoopy in various poses. This worked wonderfully when writing notes to potential dates. A Snoopy added to a query got you several rungs up the dating ladder. The half of my brain in charge of anything to do with mathematics was certain that math was Satan's domain. Geometry was invented by a Greek who was pissed off because his restaurant went under, and Physics should be left to Einstein and Tesla.

High school for me was a happy time. The school was divided into three groups: the Jocks, the Hippies, and the Bandies. Having grown up minus the influence of video games, baseball, touch football and basketball were all we had, and we loved it. I was a drummer in grade school and middle school but dropped the school band route to join a garage band. Subbing for another band in 1967 when I was fifteen, we played a frat party at Lehigh. Calling it an eye opener would be an understatement. I matured several years that night. Because of my athletic and music abilities and my penchant for playing the clown, I could vacillate among all three groups. While my long hair and wire rims didn't put off the Jocks, it endeared me to the musicians. A lifelong credo began to emerge for me: a life spent making people smile or laugh has no bad side effects and many perks. Karma…what you send out…you receive in return.

The odyssey of life after high school, in truth, began one bright cool autumn day in 1969. I had fulfilled most of my requirements for graduation, so I was given several study halls to fill up my schedule. Having mastered the art of sleeping with my eyes open by early October, I was suddenly awakened by Mr. Webb, our study hall proctor.

Mr. Webb was a geometry teacher, but also a very good pistol shooter and a World War II vet. In no small way I believe I had made it through his geometry classes by loaning him my latest copy of "Guns and Ammo" magazine, which he read in the teachers' lounge. Now he was tapping me on the shoulder and handing me a yellow slip. Looking down at the gun magazine next to me, he gave me a rueful smile and said, "Mr. Neff, how does a hippie come to like guns and hunting?" Actually, I liked guns but not hunting. I had hunted when I was fourteen. I shot a rabbit and had held it as it cried, dying. "I only shoot paper targets….they don't bleed." He smiled and walked away. The note was from the guidance office. Mr. Fuhr requested my presence. I headed slowly up the stairs to the second floor.

I had served the previous year as a messenger for the guidance office, so I knew this was the "What are you planning to do with your life, son" discussion. Usually this was reserved for juniors, but after getting to know me the previous year, for some reason Mr. Fuhr had postponed meeting with me as long as he could. My course of study had been college prep, only because the list was small and "Bethlehem Steel prep" wasn't on it. His door opened, he looked out, sighed, and said "I'll see you now, Mr. Neff." I walked in, sat down, and he asked me what I planned on doing with my life. He already knew that my father and my brothers worked at Bethlehem Steel. "Well, sir, I've narrowed it down to two possibilities: a mercenary or a cat burglar." Mr. Fuhr was neither stunned nor affronted. Instead he smiled and said "Get the hell out of my office." I obliged, but as I was closing the door he said, "Mr. Neff, Bethlehem Steel is a dangerous place. Be careful."

Recently I have tried to think how many times in my working career I've heard that phrase. Not "be careful," but "Get the hell out of my office." And my career goal was set. Work anywhere until

I got "the call". Hopefully the fix was in.

1970 was a pivotal year in creating the person I am today. It was also one of the most wonderful years of my life. Most of my belief systems were shaped in the latter half of that year. My ideologies on music, religion, politics, ecology and war all seemed to coalesce.

Upon entering high school in the fall of 1967, my views on the war in Vietnam were relatively hawkish. I believed, as many did, that we were there to stop the spread of Communism. After three years of seeing through the political rhetoric, watching the war on television, and the war protests, I became disillusioned. I spoke to many Vietnam veterans who told me what it was really like. The massacre at Kent State was the defining point which changed me forever. Having turned eighteen in November, the only distressing problem in my future was that I was eligible for the draft. Having been raised with the values of the time with words like honor, duty, and patriotism, I found it hard to join the ranks of draft card burners. I decided I would wait for the lottery and take my chances. With four years of German studies behind me, I reasoned that if I were drafted, I might be able to do my tour in Europe. Ironic to think this, because my original reason for studying German was to understand what the Nazi soldiers were saying on the TV show Combat.

During this time, I was working on the grounds crew at a nursing home in West Bethlehem, a job which I held throughout high school. Earning $1.50 per hour, I realized I wasn't going to afford that Maserati I had drooled over at Watkins Glen. In October 1970 I had taken a road trip up there to see the Grand Prix with my friend Bob Palmer. Bob and I were friends from high school. He was the lead guitarist in our garage band in high school. He was an exemplary guitar player, and our band practiced a lot, but had dissolved in 1968.

Our trip was a learning experience to say the least. Upon arriving on a Saturday, we realized that October in the Finger Lakes region of New York can get quite a bit colder than Pennsylvania. We decided to check out some of the cars that would be in the race on Sunday. We are now in the middle of a parking lot with about three thousand others who are all in various states of being stoned or well oiled. If you've never been in the middle of a crowd shoulder to shoulder, it can be quite unnerving.

No one ever knew who started it, but the back of the crowd started pushing. From experience, I always assumed it was the beer drinkers because stoners get too laid back to push. The entire crowd became like a human wheat field in a strong wind. I had an advantage, being 6'3", that I could see over the crowd. I was next to a father with two small children who were hysterical. I picked up his son and he grabbed his daughter and we worked our way over to a New York State police car. We climbed on top and he jumped over the fence. I handed his children over to him. Now I'm alone, standing on a police car, with a thousand people clapping and cheering. The last thing I wanted to be that night was a long-haired guy wearing wire rimmed glasses, and a field jacket with a peace sign on it. I turn around to see the largest New York State police officer I had ever seen holding the largest riot baton in his left hand and the largest 357 Magnum in his right hand.

He never said a word. Thankfully, the father I had helped explained what we did and the officer motioned for me to jump over the fence. I went back to thank him and all he said was "Son, don't climb on any more police cars this weekend." My lifelong respect for law and order had been established that night, as was my susceptibility to migraines. Trying to sleep on the back seat of a '62 Oldsmobile on a cold New York night does not help to diminish a migraine. We fired up the Olds and rolled into Corning. We stopped in front of the glassworks so I could evacuate everything I had eaten for the last twelve hours. Unbelievably, we found the only motel room in Corning, vacated by an expectant mother whose due date had arrived. Bob conjured up some Anacin for me, we slept for a few hours, and headed back for the race.

In the last 48 hours I had frozen, starved, been trampled, was almost shot, and had experienced the worst headache in my life. Only years later would I think of this as my baptism of fire, training camp for working thirty years as a Bethlehem Steel rigger.

The trip did have some wonderful outcomes. Riding down 181 south of Binghamton was the first time I heard "Fire and Rain" by James Taylor on the car radio. I arrived home starving and found that my loving and remarkable mother had left me a plate of pot roast, potatoes, peas and applesauce. That was, without equal, the best meal I had in my entire life. Bless her Irish heart. The last wonderful thing that happened was that I finally got a date with Carol.

Dating in high school is where relationships usually consist of steaming up car windows, meeting parents, and going to Burger King after Friday football games. These encounters never last much more than a few weeks, two months at most. I was more of a loner, so I usually waited until I heard a rumor that someone liked me and was open for a date. I eventually developed the courage to start asking girls on dates. This was about the same time I graduated. I'm still making $1.50 an hour and using my father's car for dating.

Then I met Carol. She was a very pretty young junior at BecaHi when we met. She had a wonderful sense of humor. We spent a lot of time together. Double dating with Dan and Lisa, we ate a lot of pizza at Toby's in Nazareth and smoked a lot of Tareyton filters. We hung out at the Rose Garden on Bethlehem's West Side, listening to the songs of the late sixties and early seventies. Carol opened up a lot of untapped emotions which I had never felt before. Looking back I can honestly say it was the first time I fell in love.

In 1970 I had also become an avid hiker, backpacker and novice rock climber, and was into the first months of my climbing career. I had accumulated some technical gear and a good solid Austrian climbing rope. The gear and ropes were still fairly inexpensive because the climbing boom of the eighties and nineties hadn't arrived yet. I had everything I needed to excel at climbing: I had no fear of heights. I was tall, thin and agile, with a mindset like every eighteen year old that you are indestructible; and I had a driving desire to succeed at everything I tried. What I didn't have was a climbing partner, so most of my early climbs were what are called "free climbs".

It is strange, sometimes, how we are affected by external stimuli, and the sixties and seventies abounded with them. Music, politics, religion, racism, civil rights, war, the ERA, ecology and not the least of all, the sexual revolution which I must say I embraced with open arms. "Free love" was everywhere.

On a weekend backpacking trip with a buddy of mine, we were hiking a section of the Appalachian Trail in May of 1971.

Hiking west we soon ran into two young ladies who were hiking east. We decided to camp in the same area. After supper one of the ladies lit up a joint, so we passed it around. A few hours later we were all buzzed, watching the campfire die. One of the ladies gets up, takes my hand and we walk into the shadows. She asks me if I would like to share her tent for the night.

"No problem. But what about my friend?"

"Oh, that's not a problem. He can sleep with my friend," she said.

Arrangements made, we retired to our respective tents. In the morning we were packing up the gear and were ready to head out. We had camped out that night directly above the Lehigh Tunnel where the Appalachian Trail crosses it. We kissed them goodbye and they headed east as we headed west. Before they travelled too far, I turned back and yelled "Hey girls! What are your names?" My partner laughed and said "I'm Patty and she's Trish." She smiled and waved. As for me, I never had a problem with that night, but my friend was Catholic and had a lot of fessing up to do.

In my younger years growing up, my parents had instilled in my brothers, sisters and me a belief in a higher power and to live our lives to high moral standards. We belonged to a Baptist church, but did not attend regularly. For the first eighteen years of my life I looked into various doctrines and beliefs. On a cold, pre-Christmas night I went out on a date with Carol. One of her school friends invited us to a party in Bethlehem. After the usual rounds of Christmas well-wishing, her friend took us up to her room to listen to an album called "Jesus Christ Superstar". Since its conception by Andrew Lloyd Weber and Tim Rice in 1969 and its eventual release in 1970, it had been attacked and vilified by many Christian clergymen. The Catholic Church had taken the lead in these attacks and woe to the parishioner who owned a copy. None of my Jewish friends seemed to have a problem with it.

Listening to it ignited something inside of me. While some might say that not all of my future adventures were quite in synch with what organized religion had in mind, Weber and Rice's music and lyrics led me to feel that simple Belief was all it took, and that I should live my life without dumping on anyone. Do no harm. So at eighteen I had my basic life tenets established. Now it was time to get a job.

Even though I had assumed that "the fix was in" at the Bethlehem Steel, job openings there had dried up in 1970. There had been a fairly large hiring wave in 1969, and now the only new job postings were rare and required special skills that I didn't have. But during our weekend at Watkins Glen my buddy Bob had persuaded me to apply for a job at the Oldsmobile dealership where he worked. It would be a 25 cent an hour raise in pay.

2 CITY MOTORS

I made my move from my nursing home job to City Motors, an Oldsmobile dealership on East Broad Street in Bethlehem, in early 1971. My friend Bob picked me up on a cold, snowy day in early January and off we headed for my first day.

At City Motors, I was to be the company "go for". I was to go to other dealerships or parts stores for parts or deliver repaired cars to customers.

Now Dave, the boss, asks me "Larry, you can drive a standard transmission truck, can't you?"

"Uh….yeah," I said, and headed over to the Parts Department, where Bob worked. I looked at him and said "Stick shift. You never said this job required me to drive stick."

"Look, we have to go over to Krick's Bakery to pick up donuts for the mechanics. I'll teach you." He gave me a ten-minute lesson on driving a '65 Dodge pickup truck with a three-speed stick shift on the column in a raging snow storm. Talk about stress! He managed to teach me enough so I could drive far enough away from the dealership, so I wouldn't look like a jackass. Within about three days I became quite proficient with the Dodge, and soon I was driving around all over Allentown and Bethlehem in a beat-up pickup, eating donuts, drinking coffee, smoking Marlboros and listening to Chicago, CSNY, the Stones and Carole King. God….I'm living the dream.

About two weeks into my new job, a mechanic called "The

Reb" sold me my first car, a two-toned 1959 Oldsmobile Rocket 88, for twenty five dollars. The interior was the size of a two-bedroom Cape Cod and it was slightly under the gross weight of a WWII aircraft carrier. The body was comprised mostly of Detroit rust held together by duct tape and, I believe, hairspray. I found six empty cans of Aqua-Net on the back seat. As I left the lot, the Reb smiled and said "If you get it up to fifty MPH, don't stab the brake too hard. The frame will stop, but the body might keep going."

My first car.......I was the captain, navigator, and mechanic of five tons of Detroit Iron on bald tires. I would dock it up the street when picking my girlfriend Carol up for a date so her parents wouldn't see it. This was a few years before OPEC stuck it to us. Gas was 37 cents a gallon and motor oil was cheap.

I was about four months into my job and starting to feel like it was time to move on. Little did I know, the events of the next few days would reinforce that notion.

One cold rainy day in early April, I'm cruising up Union Blvd in Allentown with a parts delivery. I'm following a semi, hauling pigs to the A&B meat packing plant. They seemed happy, sticking their noses through the open slats in the trailer. Poor bastards! They didn't have any idea they would be on shelves at the Acme in a few days. During this time we're sitting at the stop light at Airport Road adjacent to the old Walp's Diner. The semi pulled out so I stayed about two feet off of his tail. Just as I was about to give the pigs a "vaya con dios" wave, the semi hit its brakes. I steam rolled the company pickup truck into the back of the trailer.

I learned two things at that moment. Pigs are capable of laughter, and never use your own vehicle to tailgate. The ICC rail on the back of the trailer tore off the pickup's front bumper and pushed the radiator and fan into the block. I managed to get the Dodge back to the dealership, all the while wondering where I could apply for a new job.

I walk into the office and see the owner, my boss, and the parts manager. It's just a formality. "You're terminated. Turn in your keys."

"C'mon guys.....Lighten up. At least the pigs had a good laugh."

"Get the hell out of my office."

Four months. Not enough time invested for a pension plan. I'll worry about that later.

So, with the unbridled optimism of a nineteen-year-old, I embarked on a quest for my next full-time position.

3 CHAIN BIKE

My next employment was with the Chain Bike Corp. It was a bicycle manufacturing company based in Rockaway NY, with a satellite plant in Hanover Township. We constructed and assembled Ross bicycles, including a very reliable fifteen-speed road bike.

I was working in the shipping department at the end of the assembly line. I worked with a partner, Brian, putting boxes over bike frames coming off the line. We would work for two to three hours at a time, rhythmically and methodically packing bikes. I only hope by now that automated robots do this.

Another guy on the line was a Lehigh University graduate who confided in me one day not that long after I had started, that his dream was to ride one of those bikes straight to Denver and open a leather shop making belts and moccasins. He was accumulating an entire bike, piece by piece. He rode off one clear summer day, never to be seen again. I really hope he made it.

Chain Bike was the first job that I ever had where I kept a list on my nightstand of excuses for calling off of work. I had the usuals, such as "Car broke down". I was still driving the Rocket 88 and this excuse wasn't exactly unbelievable. But you could have fired an armor piercing round through the engine block and it would still have run. My all-time favorite excuse was the infrequently used but always dreaded conjunctivitis, or to the layman, "pink eye". Just say you have pink eye, and your co-workers are running for the exits. I imparted this nugget of wisdom to one of the guys working on the line. He was always stoned and his eyes were always red. Occasionally, he would use "get the red out" eye drops on one eye, and then would show his boss his other, always bloodshot eye. A free afternoon off. He finally overdid it and tried it once too many times. The boss handed him a termination slip and said, "Read it with your good eye, son."

One day at break time Brian motioned me to follow him out to the loading dock. He started climbing the ladder on a boxcar. I followed him up and when we got on top, there were about a dozen workers sitting up there listening to music and smoking pot. It took a few coffee breaks for me to get my first buzz, but in a few days boxing bicycles didn't seem so bad. Coffee breaks were fantastic.

The workforce was multi-racial, so there were blacks, whites, Hispanics, Asians, Native Americans, all being nice to one another. It was beautiful. It was like that "I'd like to sing" Coke commercial, but the closest thing to a coke bottle was a bong being passed around. The guy who owned it was a Vietnam vet, who kept the bong in a camouflaged bag in a nearby tree. Sitting on a boxcar, catching rays, smoking a joint and eating Ring Dings. I'm living the dream.

One beautiful summer day, just after lunch, I was jacking a boxcar that had just been loaded away from the docking ramp. We had a long pole with a wedge and wheel on the end. With it, one man could move a five ton boxcar. My partner for the day was Juan. His job was to climb up and release the brake wheel, and then come back down and block the car wheel when it was in position. The railroad tracks were a two mile incline up to the loading dock. Conrail engines would bring up the cars, but it was up to the shipping crew to adjust them. As I jacked the car, it started to roll down the track, picking up speed as it went. Unfortunately Juan was lighting up a joint as the car rolled by him. By now it was rolling too fast to block, so we decided on the only thing that we could possibly do. The eight people working the dock started singing, "na na na na, hey hey hey, goodbye." Juan's laughing, and turns around to see Sam the shipping boss eyeballing him. Now Sam weighed in at about 280 pounds and seemed to be nine feet tall, even when we weren't stoned. Being Jamaican, he had always been okay with the toking, but he didn't like screw-ups. So, as Danny the dock boss had frequently reiterated, "Don't screw up and Sam won't crush your head like a grape." Unfortunately we now had a major screw-up, and Sam had Juan locked in his sights. Juan stopped laughing and started running, with Sam right behind him. Danny looked back at the rest of us, and said "Poor bastard....does anybody know if Juan has a family?" We lost it.

A few days before the conclusion of my third full-time position, Sam pulled me aside and told me that I was needed to work the parts packaging job. A young girl named Brenda usually did it, but she had gone home sick. She was a sweet girl whose job was to package all of the nuts, bolts, reflectors and decals for the bikes coming off the line. She was good at her job, most probably because she never got high. Now I had the job, and Sam told me we had five hundred bikes coming off the line. I honestly did begin with the best intentions of doing a proper job, but there were three mitigating circumstances working against me. It was Friday. It was pay day. I was high.

It took me ten minutes to get over my fascination with the heat seal machine which was used to close the parts bags. Normally it would have escaped my notice but remember, I was high. I had to see what it would do to a Snickers bar. After ten minutes of testing other objects and finding out that the machine made no distinction between a plastic bag and a human finger, I painfully started collecting the parts to be packaged.

To my credit, I must say that at least fifty correct bags of parts went into the boxes of the first run. Then I entered the uncontrollable laughing stage. I became less and less diligent as to what parts were going into which bags. One sealed bag went into a box containing only two axle nuts and a broken reflector that I had accidentally stepped on. One bag's sealed contents contained a rather malformed and melted Snickers bar. A few bags went out with a handwritten note which featured a cartoon dog stating "We are undergoing a parts shortage and are waiting for a shipment from Taiwan." Some had notes with smiley faces and the ever-present "have a nice day".

At this time I was not aware of the discipline of Karma: what you send out into the universe, you will receive in return. Whatever entity controls Karma must have shown incalculable mercy toward me. Many years later, putting toys and bikes together for my sons, it seems I always had the right parts and hardware. Unlike Karma, however, Big Sam showed very little mercy. I was called to his office first thing Monday morning. All he said was "You're a hard worker, but I must let you go." "Why?" I asked. Big Sam reached into his drawer, smiled, and pulled out a plastic bag containing a maltreated Snickers bar.

With thoughts of my declining batting average and my brain slightly altered by the effects of cannabis and an ever-growing talent for mischievousness, I set my sights on a new position.

4 FREIHOFFERS BAKERY

The Steel company still wasn't hiring, so my next attempt at gainful employment (which I remember as "the hot bread zombie tour"), was with Freihoffers Bakery on Union Boulevard in East Allentown. I chose it because it was within walking distance of home in West Bethlehem, and it was getting harder and harder to wake up my Rocket 88 to get me to work. Most days I would let it sleep in, but on days I was late I had to use it. It would inevitably leave a puddle of oil in the parking lot to show its disdain for my audacity in using it to propel me somewhere.

I was called in for an interview and a tour only one day after applying. This led me to believe that they were desperate. I could smell the baked bread a mile away when I arrived for my interview. I pondered whether my destiny was baking bread. The warmth of the oven and the smell of the bread took me back to a time when I would sit on my mother's lap waiting for bread or cookies to magically appear. I met some gentleman in a suit who interviewed me. It seemed to me that the one qualification you were required to have to be hired was that you were breathing. Then came the tour. It was thoroughly depressing. The ovens were probably built in the early 1900's, with newer technology added on in later years. The entire workplace looked like a cross between Willy Wonka's chocolate factory and something Edgar Allen Poe would concoct in one of his darker moods. Of course it was a warm day in August and the heat of the ovens only added to the suffocating atmosphere of the place. We finally came to the end of this massive oven, with the doors open, to see several hundred loaves of bread moving slowly toward us. With unabashed pride my tour guide smiles and points to a large sign over the oven door. "This is the largest bread oven in the free world."

How they came to this conclusion was a mystery to me. Did someone travel the entire length and breadth of the Soviet Union, Soviet bloc, Cuba and Red China with a foot rule, checking all of their ovens? Did the CIA have pictures of the heat blooms of all the Communist bread ovens from overflying U2 spy planes, or maybe that wacko Senator McCarthy toured the plant in the 1950's and the sign was erected just to placate him? I suppose no one knows, but they were very proud of it.

The only thing that bothered me during the tour was that all the employees wore white uniforms with little pointed white hats: the kind of hats that look like you're wearing a large white airmail envelope on your head. You could possess an IQ of 180 and if you wore a hat like that you would look like a blockhead. I was offered the job, so it came down to accepting a job where it would be eternally hot, I'd be working twelve hour shifts, and I would look like an ice cream vendor. The only upside to this was the starting wage of $3.75 per hour. With the minimum wage still at $1.50 per hour, I would be making almost as much as my father was making at Bethlehem Steel. I accepted the position. It was a Thursday, so I had three days until I was to start my first shift on Monday at 5 AM.

I have never believed in omens, but after that weekend I started believing. With a long weekend ahead of me, I decided to do some climbing. Most climbers today know the best places to go: Stovers State Park in Bucks County and the "Gunks" in upstate New York. In the early seventies there were a few places around Bethlehem where one could practice. One was the thirty to forty foot rock faces at the south edge of Nisky Hill Cemetery. At the bottom of the cliff face was a rarely-used railroad spur which had a track to deliver coal to the Fritch Fuel Company on Sand Island. Since most homeowners had switched over to natural gas or oil to heat their homes in the early seventies, it was uncommon to see a train on that spur. So, on a beautiful warm Saturday morning I walked down to that area and started climbing one of the easier rock faces, with numerous handholds and footholds.

I had successfully ascended to about twenty five or thirty feet when I reached to a handhold about eighteen inches above my head. At the same time I see a slow-chugging diesel train pulling about three or four coal cars below me. I reach up to that handhold which was a ledge about ten inches deep. As I put my hand up and feel for a hold, I suddenly wonder to myself, "Who left a plate of linguini up here? No wait...Linguini doesn't move by itself." I still hadn't realized what it was until I jammed my right hand in a vertical crack, got a new foothold and pulled myself up to look over the edge. As I peer over the edge, I'm staring at a rather pregnant garter snake, giving birth to about twenty or thirty offspring.

As repulsive as this seemed to me, my first conscious thought at the time was "Why the fuck did you think it was a plate of linguini, you moron?" This is where the wonder of the human mind kicks in. I am thirty feet up on a rock face, between a mound of baby snakes and a moving train which is shaking the hell out of everything. If you panic you perish. At that moment two things must have happened. My brain must have pumped out one big shitload of endorphins and it was the first time in my short life that I actually needed physical aid from my guardian angel. He, she or it probably thought "This yoyo has done some really stupid things in his life, but this tops them all." Whatever it was, a sudden calm came over me. I traversed over to the right a few feet, and climbed the remaining fifteen feet to the top, where reality set in and I lost most of my breakfast. As I lay there with my face half submerged in my former meal, I had no way of realizing that this was a training run on my way to becoming a Bethlehem Steel rigger.

After spending a nice Sunday with Carol, I woke at 4 AM full of optimism for starting my new job. Fortunately, we could change into our ill-fitting lily white uniforms at work and wouldn't have to be subjugated to the wisecracks if we actually had to wear them in public. I met some of my coworkers in the break room and was introduced to my partner that morning. They all seemed to be walking zombies due to the twelve hour workday shifts which constantly changed due to mechanical problems. My co-worker Bobby seemed to be a nice guy. He was in his forties at the time, and I found out after working a few days that he had a rather large family with several children. We worked together at the end of the bread oven. When the bread was exiting the oven, there were three loaves in each tray, riding a conveyer line to our workstation. An overhead monorail ran parallel to us on our left side with five or six long carts suspended from it next to us. As the trays came out they ran under a machine that looked like a mechanical octopus tentacle. It would rotate and suck the bread out of the trays, sending the bread to packaging and the trays over to us. Our only job was to stack the trays on the carts and send them to get cleaned. The job wasn't really that bad. You didn't have to be a rocket scientist to do it, and it had nice break times. You were expected to work around the baking times, so you might have a two-hour break but then work for three hours.

From my first day I rebelled against wearing those stupid hats. Occasionally, a suit from the office would come by with a tour and would ask me where my hat was. I'd point to the tours and ask him where their hats were. The suit would frown and walk away. I must have had an AFL/CIO Union logo stamped into my DNA, a result of my father being a lifelong union member, but in reality my non-compliance was just my aversion to looking stupid. From the first day I learned that if I leaned over at my workstation and got too close to the pneumatic bread sucker, it would actually suck your hat from your head. It seems that even pneumatic bread sucking machines are endowed with a fashion conscience. Bobby would get a laugh out of watching the hat getting sucked off my head and would bring other employees to see it. Actually, nobody ever knew where the hats went. I suppose they slipped into a parallel universe, or perhaps it was the "lost sock in the dryer" phenomenon. Either way, the "hat trick" was short-lived. One of the bosses saw it. I suppose that was the first chink in the armor of my having a long career. In actuality, I knew that this job could never be my fate after working the first week, so I resigned myself to the fact that my end as a bakery worker was drawing near.

The last blow came one night in late August, and I really had no control over it. It was about 3 AM on an unexpectedly cool morning for a day in August. We were on a break between baking cycles and I was standing by a window on the Union Blvd. side of the building watching the people sitting in Mr. Donut. As I was pondering their situation, deciding whether they were nightshift workers or insomniacs, Bobby came by.

To understand what happened next, you need to know that around the time I began work there, the federal government had passed consent decree laws that required compensation for workers who had been held back from advancement due to race. This had nothing to do with my position, but I had listened to Bobby complain that he had been expecting to move up to the riser machine position but had been passed over by an employee who had emigrated from Lebanon the year before.

The job working on the riser was much easier than what Bobby and I were doing. It was entirely automated. You merely sat there, making sure that the machine functioned properly. You could drink coffee, read magazines, and listen to the radio. In the machine, rolls of bread would slide down a chute falling into the bread pans. One roll per pan. Then it would be a short ride by conveyor into the riser.

Bobby comes up to me and says, "We're going up to the riser. Keep the operator busy, I've got something to do."

So we go up there and I start talking to the guy, asking him how he likes his new job. With his heavy accent, it was all I could do to understand him. As we were talking, I look over to see Bobby stuffing five or six rolls of dough into one pan. With three pans per tray, he's sending about eighteen loaves of bread in one tray into the riser. He pulls an empty off the line and replaces it with the rigged one. Then he comes over to me, grabs my arm, and says "Let's get back to work."

I was smart enough to know what was happening but I reasoned that it wouldn't come back to me. All I did was talk to the operator. I'm out of the loop on this one. About an hour later, all hell breaks loose. Lights are flashing, sirens wailing, people running everywhere. Everybody is running over to the oven. Bobby and I were scheduled to start stacking pans in about fifteen minutes, so we headed over.

When we got there, about sixty people were lined up abreast, looking into the oven. When I looked in, I saw a loaf of bread about half of the way back, stuck in the oven. It was the size, and remarkably like the shape of a Volkswagen Beetle. It started to catch on fire. The gas was shut off and maintenance guys had to crawl in with hooks to pull it out. I turned around to look at Bobby. He didn't look happy. Actually, he never was very bright. Now he looked like a man with a big family who realized he had done something very stupid.

The investigation started the next day. Bobby got called in first. Then it was my turn. The headhunters were looking for a head. They had lost six hundred loaves of bread because of that stunt. I go in and sit down, and they ask me what happened. I have no idea what Bobby has told them, so I just say "I don't know anything about it."

Bobby must have sold me out. I felt no animosity toward him. For him it was survival and for me it was just another job that I really didn't like. Something else would turn up, or the Steel Company would call. Without much fanfare I was let go and Bobby remained. But on the way out, I turned back and said "At least one good thing came out of this."

They looked at me and someone said "What."

"Now you can make a new sign. We have the largest fuckin loaf of fuckin bread in the Free Fuckin World." The secretary that was taking notes burst out laughing, so they were glaring at her when I closed the door.

5 THE HOSPITAL

"Would you like me to teach you how to ski?" That question changed my life forever! It was a cold winter evening in mid-March 1972. I was standing by a window at the time clock at 4:55 on a cold Monday, watching a light snow falling on the cars in the parking lot. I heard soft footsteps behind me, so I turned and met the gaze of the softest, prettiest green Irish eyes. They belonged to Margaret, Maggie to her friends.

"Isn't it beautiful," she said, standing close to me, looking out of the window. "Yes," I agreed. "I love walking home in it."

"You don't have a car?" she asked.

"Well, I had a '59 Oldsmobile, but it died recently, so I'm walking a lot lately."

"Where do you live?" she asked.

"On the West Side, around 12th Avenue."

"That's quite a hike," she said. "I'd be happy to give you a ride." I quickly accepted and while she was warming up the car, in the soft glow of the dashboard lights, I took my first good look at her. Long, fine red hair, beautiful soft smooth skin without make-up. Her figure under her nurse's uniform was slightly full, but shapely. I guessed she was probably in her late thirties. Although she was twenty years my senior, I made that instant deep biological connection to her. As she drove me home we chatted about the usual things. She asked me about my hobbies. I told her that I was into mostly outdoor endeavors: hiking, backpacking and climbing.

"Do you ski?" she asked.

"Just cross-country, never tried downhill."

"I love downhill skiing!" By this time she had dropped me off and I walked around to her side of the car to thank her. She looked up at me with those eyes. "I rented a cabin for this weekend at Camelback. Would you like me to teach you how to ski?" In my nineteen years on this planet I had never felt before what she had just done to me with that simple question and coy smile. I desperately summoned up all of the unruffled self-assurance that I could lay hold of.

"I would love that." I told her I worked until five on Friday.

"Great, so do I. I'll meet you at the time clock, and we can leave from there." As her tail lights disappeared into the falling snow, I stood there wondering if what had just happened was real, or was Rod Serling going to walk up to me with a cigarette in his mouth and say "There's a signpost up ahead, and you have just entered the Twilight Zone."

This story actually begins in September of 1971, when I was hired at St. Luke's Hospital. Back then it wasn't a mega-hospital with satellite sites all over the Lehigh Valley. This was before all the advances in technology. No MRIs, no lasers, no surgical robots. It was before paramedics and Medivac flights. If you were unfortunate enough to find yourself lying on the highway after an accident, you were grabbed, thrown on a stretcher, and shoved into the back of a Cadillac. You were then driven like a bat out of hell to the E.R., dragged out, x-rayed until you glowed, and then sliced open, repaired, sewn up and laid in a room for two weeks until they released you.

In this archaic medical world I found myself working as an orderly in the operating theater, which was situated on the ninth floor of the North Wing. The job was split between being an "outside orderly" or an "inside orderly". Outside orderlies brought patients up from their rooms when they were scheduled for surgery, then took them back after they left the recovery room. You took biopsy samples to the lab, and delivered amputated appendages and former surgical patients who didn't make it to the basement morgue. If you were scheduled as an "inside orderly" the duties were completely different. You had to suit up in the locker room in the same scrubs as the surgeons or the surgical nurses: green scrub pants and shirt, hair cover, mask, and shoe covers. Inside orderlies moved patients into the OR suites and up onto the operating tables. After surgical procedures were performed, you got to remove the suction materials and other dubious foul-smelling items, and cleaned and sterilized the rooms. You did this with the aid of the OR porter (or janitor.) Shifts went fast working inside the OR because with eight operating rooms all functioning simultaneously, you really kept moving. Occasionally you got to watch a surgical procedure, which was always interesting. But you always longed to be an outside orderly.

Shifts working as an outside orderly were generally boring, but easier than working inside. As long as you kept a close eye on the surgical schedule for that particular day and all the patients prepped for surgery made it to the OR fifteen minutes before their scheduled time, no one bothered you. The long interims between duties meant you whiled away your time in the employee lounge, smoking cigarettes, drinking coffee or paging through the usual medical magazines, tearing out the cigarette coupons. If you happened to be low on smokes you would venture into the doctors locker room. They would leave their smokes on the bench when showering. This was rarely done, with cigarettes at 45 cents a pack. Most of the time you could ask a doctor for a smoke and he would give you one, after explaining the dangers of smoking to you. "Hey Doc, why don't you quit?" you would ask, and the usual reply would be "I've been smoking for forty years, son. It's too late for me to quit." Even after viewing surgeries of cancerous lung removals you'd go back to the lounge to light up. "I'll smoke for a couple more years and then quit." No fear of death with nineteen year olds. They live forever. This is where I met Hiram. He was a few years older than me and one of the hippest guys I have ever met. Hiram could tell at a glance who liked cannabis and who didn't. About two weeks after starting work at the hospital I began hanging out with Hiram and some of the other orderlies at Hiram's room, which was rented to him by the hospital. It was in an ancient wing which was later demolished to build the Doctors pavilion and parking deck, just east of the North Wing. We'd all get high listening to Santana, Hendrix, Cream, and Traffic. (Just recently I downloaded Traffic's fantastic eleven minute rendition of "The Low Spark of High-Heeled Boys". It was the first time I had ever heard it when I wasn't stoned.)

We all kicked in to pay for the pot and I never asked where it came from, nor ever carried it on my person. I didn't want to wind up doing thirty years for having a nickel bag and zig zag papers in my pocket. One night just before Christmas, we broke up the after-work party and everyone was heading out the door. Hiram stops me and hands me a small Ziploc bag with two expertly rolled joints and an alligator clip for the roaches. I was about to do something I never did: carry some weed on me and smoke at home. Prior to this I always confined getting stoned to the workplace. So I slip him a few bucks and start heading home. I had begun walking the three miles to work because the beast, my Rocket 88, had finally succumbed to the inevitable. It had surpassed the normal death age of Detroit Iron by many years, even though we were in the days of planned obsolescence. This was when cars were built to last two or three years. Then you traded it in and bought a new one. My Iron Rocket lasted twelve. My father had arranged to have it put down when I was at work. It was towed to a bone yard, smelted down, shipped overseas and probably turned into three or four Datsuns. Going home from work was a bit easier than going to work. Back then, there was much more rail traffic than now. I simply waited by the railroad trestle where the trains had to negotiate a turn, which made them slow down.

This is where a lesson my father had taught me came to be valuable. When he was a young boy in Missouri, he and some of his friends were hopping a freight train to go swimming. One boy grabbed the back ladder, lost his grip, then lost his leg falling between the cars. Most fathers would have made the moral of this story, "Don't hop trains." My dad knew me well, and instead always told me if you hop a train, grab the front ladder on the car in the direction it is travelling. If the momentum of the train makes you lose your grip, you'll swing against the car and fall away from the train. After hopping a train, I would ride it out to 11th or 12th Avenue and walk home. Two miles by rail, one mile by foot.

At that time I was living in an apartment with my parents. When I arrived home, my mother was watching television and my father was working. It was about seven o'clock, so after telling my mom I had a headache, I retired to my room and locked the door. I took my window fan out and put it in the window backwards. I then proceeded to smoke both joints and blow the smoke out through the fan. Now most early users of cannabis don't think anyone can notice its pungent odor. I sent enough smoke out of that window that bloodhounds in West Virginia could smell it.

Then came the inevitable munchies. When they hit, you are transformed into the supreme eating machine. You will consume almost anything: car bumpers, furniture, railroad ties or slow-moving animals. I have always wondered why most pot smokers don't weigh 400 pounds. My favorite munchies were Screamin Yellow Zonkers or Tastykake chocolate cupcakes.

After airing out my room, I came out and told my mother I was going over to the 7-Eleven to get something to eat. "I just made a chocolate cake", she said. It was sitting on the counter. Not wanting her to get suspicious, I ate half of it, while drinking a quart of milk. She looked at me and said "Are you drunk?" I don't think, in the entire history of humans, that anyone has ever fooled their mother. Suspecting that being drunk was more socially acceptable to her than being stoned, I simply nodded and left. When I got to the 7-Eleven, a ten minute trip which seemed to take two hours, I was mortified to find they were out of Zonkers. I proceeded to deliver a twenty minute dissertation to the counter girl on the importance of reordering while you still have stock on the shelves. I left with six three-packs of TastyKake chocolate cupcakes and a gallon of chocolate milk, which all disappeared on the way home. With a distended abdomen and a pancreas working overtime, I stumbled into bed and fell fast asleep. I woke up with a raging migraine six hours later, with another life lesson learned.

Very quickly into a new job I could pick out the employees who were into marijuana. They all possessed the minute, tell-tale signs. Easier to detect were the nonsmokers. There were two kinds of these: the kind who would smile and look the other way, and the narcs. The narcs were the ones with bloodhound noses ready to drop a dime on you.

Hank was a porter in the OR. He was doing one year of hospital service after filing as a conscientious objector with the draft board. He was one of the coolest guys I ever worked with. He had to stay squeaky clean or the selective service board would drop his CO status and slap a 1A on him.

When we started our coffee break smoke out, we didn't invite Hank for obvious reasons. Our clandestine group would meet upstairs on the tenth floor amid the air conditioner condensers. They were loud enough to mask any activity, plus they blew the smoke away with their giant fans. It was a tight group: me, Hiram, Dale, Brian, and occasionally one or two nursing students. As long as we didn't take any longer than a normal coffee break, no one bothered us. Two drops of Visine and back to work. It ran that way for a few months, so we started pushing the envelope. We started meeting in the cystoscopic treatment room which was outside the OR suites, but adjacent to them on the ninth floor. It had a lead-lined door on the bathroom because they would occasionally do Xrays in that room. We would fit three or four people in the bathroom and lock the door. Whoever lit up would stand on the toilet and blow the smoke up into the ceiling fan. This actually worked until the laughing or giggling became too loud.

One day there were five of us in there, having a great party when someone "came a knockin'". It was the department supervisor banging on the door and screaming "I know what you're doing in there!" Roaches down the crapper, Visine in the eyes and we all roll out in front of her glaring gaze. She was a tough as nails no shit takin' ex-Navy nurse, so she just stood there waiting for an explanation. Someone blurted out "Diarrhea". We all lost it. I noticed a very small tinge of a smile. She did a perfect military about-face and left. To our surprise, no disciplinary action was ever taken. I suppose it came down to the fact that we were just a pack of misfits: low paid but well-trained misfits. I assume she didn't want to train five or six new ones.

Actually, misfits may be too harsh a term for what we were. We were well-trained, but most of us knew it was really a job going nowhere. We all had our sites set for something better. The end of my employment was coming, and when it finally arrived, it came down to a decision to choose. Until my time comes to cross over from this reality to the other side, I will always say I made the right choice.

It was a Friday, mid-March, about 12:30 in the afternoon and it was also the weekend of the ski trip. I had seen Maggie at lunch. She smiled and asked me if we were still on for the weekend. This quickly expelled all of the doubts of the previous week that this was some sort of wishful hallucination. Shaking myself back to coherence, I managed to tell her my bag was packed and I was really looking forward to the trip. She whispered in my ear "We'll have a great time" and gave me a soft kiss on the cheek. In the matter of a split second, this older, pretty, red-haired woman had turned me from a confident, not unattractive, loquacious, and hopefully enlightened male into a stumbling, babbling noodle.

Standing behind me in the cafeteria line was a retired thirty-year Navy man named "Reds" who had taken a job as an orderly when he retired. He looked at me and smiled. "Son", he said "you look like you just got hit by a bolt of lightning. If this was a bar, a shot and a beer might help."

"Don't think so, Reds, I don't drink. I smoke." Reds tapped out a Camel from his pack and handed it to me. I smiled and said, "Reds, what I smoke they don't grow in Virginia." He laughed and said "Some of my shipmates smoked that stuff but I always preferred beer."

The next few hours passed excruciatingly slowly. My relationship with Carol was slowly deflating after she had dropped the inevitable bomb, which all guys in a failing relationship eventually hear: "I think we should try dating other people." Out of all the things in a relationship that I respect and admire, honesty is the predominant one. Even though it still hurt deeply, I could see her logic. But all of the melancholy feelings from our waning relationship seemed to dissolve before the anticipated ski weekend with Maggie.

I was sitting in the small lounge outside the OR smoking a cigarette, thinking about the upcoming weekend, when I was gently prodded back into the reality of the moment. I was told one of the surgeons was doing an amputation of the lower leg of a patient, but the operation was taking longer than expected. I looked at my watch, and apprehension set in. It was 4:15 and I was going to meet Maggie at the time clock at five. The procedure for removing body parts was usually a simple one. The surgical nurse would wrap the severed end with absorbent gauze, then with brown paper. Then the entire limb was wrapped in more brown paper, and sealed in a brown plastic bag. The surgical nurse would then hand it to the outside OR orderly who would contact the morgue orderly, who would open up the morgue, take the package and dispose of it. I never knew what happened to it after that, nor did I want to know. After making the handoff, my job was complete. Normally I took my job seriously, apart from a few times when we had smoked a joint at lunch. Mostly, though, I was a dedicated employee, or as dedicated as one dollar and 95 cents per hour would get you. I had performed this duty several times, and was content this time would be no different, albeit we had a time constraint.

Sitting there chain smoking, watching the little numbers on the digital clock radio flapping down the minutes, I made the decision to bail out at 4:50. There was no way in hell I was going to miss this weekend with Maggie. I suppose that and the thoughts in my mind, realizing how bad this job really sucked, precipitated my actions over the next several minutes.

At 4:42 the electric doors to the OR suite slide open and a male surgical nurse walks out and hands me a leg, with a half-assed wrap on the bloody end and the whole mess shoved into a clear plastic bag. Being of German-Irish lineage, the pressure of the last hour quickly sent me into controlled anger: Irish temper controlled by German self-discipline. "What the fuck is this?" I asked him. "We didn't have any brown plastic bags", he said, handing it to me.

"It's dripping on the fucking floor. Who the fuck wrapped this?" I asked , realizing time was ticking away. It was about this time I lost it. He looked at me and said "I did."

"Well, fuck this fuckin job and fuck you too!" I grabbed the leg and headed for the staff elevator with twelve minutes to go. I waited two minutes, when I heard the food staff rolling food carts off on the floor below me. It was dinnertime for the patients. I realized I would never get that elevator in time. I slipped on a long, white lab coat, shoved the leg up under it, and headed over to the public elevator.

What happened next was due to the fact that I had been gifted, or cursed, whichever way you see it, with a sharp wit, honed to a fine point during my nineteen years. It was also a tribute to all the one-liner comics who all had straight men to feed them a line to respond to. Costello had Abbott, George had Gracie, and Groucho had his brothers. The elevator arrived and I was delighted to see it was empty. I punched the ground floor button. As the doors closed I relaxed just slightly, confident the elevator would get me down the nine floors without anyone else getting on. My confidence evaporated at the sixth floor when a man and his wife entered the car. I stepped politely to the left to let them on and stood in the front left side. They came in, smiled, and took their places behind me. Assuring myself that my extra appendage would remain hidden, we were passing the second floor when the package I was hiding began to bleed through my lab coat in an ever-widening spot. It was then that the woman fed me the best straight line I would ever receive. She tapped me on the shoulder and said in all earnestness, "Excuse me, doctor, I believe your back is bleeding!" Without a moment of hesitation I turned and replied "It's not my back, madam, it's only my leg," and pulled out the leg to show it to them. It was perfect timing. The doors opened and they just ran out.

Another nail in the coffin of this shitty job, I mused, but the thought vanished quickly, replaced by the stray thought that I might have a career as a stand-up comic in my future. Watching my captive audience fleeing to the exit door, my short-lived gag ended with a glance at my watch. Oh shit, six minutes to go.

I quickly removed my crimson-stained lab coat, wrapped the leg in it, and headed for the stairs to the ground floor and the morgue. Taking the steps two at a time I made the short trip to the morgue door with the speed of an Olympic gold medalist. Reaching for the door knob, I realized the door was locked. Letting out an "Oh…fuck me!" I heard a voice down the hall say "Problem?" The hospital pharmacist was looking out over his half door.

"The float orderly was supposed to open the morgue door for me. I have an amputated leg to dispose of."

"Oh. He was here five minutes ago and said it was time for his supper."

"Where does he take his break? I'm going to personally feed the son of a bitch a leg for supper."

Sensing my mood, the pharmacist prudently closed the upper half of his door and I heard him lock it.

Fuck! Three minutes to go, and I'll never make it. Just then, my luck took a turn. The staff elevator opened up just around the corner. With package in tow I caught it just as the doors were closing. I expected it to be loaded with dinner carts, but found it empty. I got on and punched the five button.

One minute to go. I'll make it. I suppose I could have told Maggie of my dilemma and she, being a nurse, would have understood. On the other hand, having told the OR scrub nurse to fuck himself, the elevator incident, and my public offer to supply dinner to the float orderly had pretty much burned all my bridges. I propped the bundle in the corner of the elevator, muttered an "adios muchacho" and pressed the G button to send the elevator to the basement, with a not-too-fervent wish that the float orderly would find it. I stepped out of the elevator to see Maggie quietly waiting for me.

"How did your day go?" she asked.

"Just another boring day," I lied.

"Well, we'll have a nice weekend". In one of the offices down the hall, a radio was playing "Love the One You're With" by Stephen Stills. Turning to me, eyes twinkling, she said "I love that song." I suppose I blushed, because she looked at me with a coy smile. We clocked out, and she took my hand as we walked to her car.

Sunday, 4 AM. Outside, the wind was blowing cold sleet against the windows of the cabin. The fire we had lit a few hours before was dying out, but still made flickering shadows on the walls. Maggie was laying beside me with her head resting gently on my right shoulder and her arm across my chest. I was softly stroking her long red hair, thinking of the warm nest we had made for ourselves during the last two days. In all that time we were totally oblivious to the outside world.

I rolled over, lit up a cigarette, and lay there quietly smoking. In a few hours we would be heading back home. Some solace came from a thought: that was one of only a few times in the vastness of the cosmos that I was in the right place at the right time. I have never looked back upon that weekend with regret or guilt.

Returning late Sunday night from our ski trip, I gazed through the car window at the falling snow turning into rain. The weather seemed to match my somber mood. A smile came to my face with the thought that, during the entire weekend, neither of us had put on a pair of skis. The ride home was a quiet one.

We both knew that a relationship with such an age difference wouldn't last. Arriving home, I pulled my pack from the car, slung it over my shoulder, and walked around to Maggie's side. When I bent down to kiss her goodbye, I noticed a tear in her eye, but she never noticed the tears in mine.

I went to work on Monday and, not wholly unexpectedly, I was summoned to the nursing office and unceremoniously sacked. I never saw Maggie again.

6 SEEKING EMPLOYMENT

After my dismissal from my job at the hospital, I did not think I would have much trouble finding another one. It was shortly after this that I realized I could apply for unemployment benefits from the state. I collected U.C. money for a few months, but this barely paid for my fast food and cigarettes. At this point I really felt that I was going nowhere. My illusion of working for high wages at Bethlehem Steel seemed to be diminishing.

My growing restlessness made me want to leave Bethlehem and search for something better. One morning at 3 AM, while watching a late night movie, I saw an advertisement for enlisting in the Army. This seemed to be exactly what I needed: discipline, which I lacked, and the chance for travel. It was also the chance to emulate my older brother Tom, who had been drafted in 1965 and became a paratrooper. Injured in a training accident, he had recovered and spent the rest of his tour in Panama. The biggest fantasy I dwelled on, however, was that having taken four years of high school German, I would surely be sent to Europe, not Southeast Asia.

Three days later, to the shock of my closest friends and after a few hits on a joint, I stepped through the doorway of the Army recruiter's office. He looked up from his desk and greeted me with a combination of amazement and subdued suspicion. With long hair, wire-rimmed glasses and a peace sign on my jacket, I looked more like a war protester than a possible recruit. In 1972, with the draft lottery in full swing, very few people were enlisting. Those with low draft lottery numbers were usually trying to join the Navy or the Air Force.

He looked up at me while shuffling papers and seemed perplexed. Handing me the enrollment test I was about to take, he said "Can I ask you what your draft number is?"

"155," I replied and added "You're probably curious as to why I'm here."

"Not really," he lied, probably thinking about the fifty dollar bonus he would get for signing me up.

He handed me the test and left the room. It took me about fifteen minutes to finish it. Walking back into the room, he graded my test and handed it to me. He smiled and said "Congratulations, you aced it!"

"Well, it really wasn't that hard," I said.

Smiling, he replied, "I suppose that's true. The Army gives you forty points up front if you can read the test and spell your name correctly."

This was the first alarm bell that sounded in my head.

"I'm taking an enlistee up to the Wilkes-Barre Army Depot where he'll take the bus to Fort Dix for basic training next Tuesday," he said. "If you want to ride up with us to take the Army physical and a few more written tests, you're welcome to."

"Okay," I agreed, "but the only thing I insist on, is I want a week to think it over if and when I pass the physical."

"Not a problem," he said, while smiling and opening the door. "I'll see you Tuesday morning, at 8 AM. Have a great weekend."

Hanging out with my friends that Saturday night, the consensus was that I was out of my fucking mind. After a few beers I was beginning to believe they were right. But I was proud of the fact that I had never backed out of anything I started, so on Tuesday I met with the recruiter and enlistee and hopped into the back seat of a dull green Plymouth with "U. S. Army" stenciled on the door.

As I watched the city pass by through the window I felt unusually sad, but was bolstered by the thought that I still had a week to think about taking the big step. The two-hour ride seemed like an eternity. We entered Wilkes-Barre which was still trying to rebuild itself after having been devastated by Hurricane Agnes six months before. It all seemed to fit into my gloomy mood.

When we reached the Depot, the enlistee headed off to the line of buses, all having the same scroll sign above the windshield: Fort Dix. I was collected by an orderly with a clipboard and shuffled off to a building for my physical exams. The building was packed with newly arrived draftees. The exams took a few hours, with most of that time spent sitting on folding chairs in hallways.

What happened next was unbelievable. I, along with two other possible enlistees were taken into a classroom with about sixty draftees. Our designation was R.A. meaning "Regular Army", while the draftees' designation was U.S. After forty minutes, when we were done with our written tests, a sergeant appeared with two government men in suits and a Marine Corps gunny sergeant. The Army sergeant moves to the front of the room and says "Any R.A.'s in this room stand up and move to the rear." The three of us got up and moved back. The sergeant then says "Everyone stand up and count off by fours." After this was done he added "All number fours come to the front of the room."

Twelve or thirteen draftees moved to the front and stood there sheepishly. The Marine gunny sergeant steps forward and barks, "Congratulations men, you have now been inducted into the United States Marine Corps."

Everyone just stood there in shock, until one of the new Marines broke down and started crying. As we were shuffling out of the classroom a soldier came over to me, dressed in green fatigues and a green baseball hat. "Are you Recruit Neff?" he asked.

"I'm Larry Neff," I replied, adding "Not a recruit yet."

A sardonic smile appeared on his face and he said "Follow me." I was escorted into an office where my recruiter was sitting behind a desk, holding a pen. There were no less than four other sergeants in the room, with the largest one positioned in front of the closed exit door, his arms folded across his chest.

Offering the pen to me, the recruiter says, "We have a bus leaving for Fort Dix in twenty minutes. All you have to do is sign here." He pointed at the paper.

I looked at him and said, "I thought we had an agreement…I wanted a week to think it over before I sign up."

A sergeant sitting on a chair to my right looks up and says "Don't you think you're man enough to join up?"

I just looked at him and said "Gimme a fucking break."

As I turned to leave and headed toward the door, the sergeant blocking it looked directly into my eyes. In that microsecond I made a snap decision and rolled the proverbial dice, thinking "If he doesn't move away from the door I'll go back and sign the enlistment paper." In that moment, my entire future would be decided by his next move. When I was only three steps away, he moved aside.

In the two hour drive home, I don't believe the recruiter said two words to me. I left him with a vague promise that I would call him the following week. I never did.

Four days later, on December 8, 1972, the Bethlehem Steel employment office called me and I was told to report to work the following Monday.

7 NEW EMPLOYEE

Viewing it for the first time, the Bethlehem Steel plant was awe-inspiring. Any anecdotal stories heard previously from family members or other plant workers paled in comparison to actually seeing the inside for the first time. Their stories also fell far short of fully describing this industrial city within a city.

The initial tour for new employees was something like a basic survival course. There were some who, after the tour, viewed it as much too dangerous and failed to return. In fact they were right: it was an extremely dangerous place to work. Everything you were introduced to seemed gargantuan. Iron-spewing blast furnaces rising hundreds of feet into the air. Giant electro-diesel railroad engines tugging submarine cars filled with three hundred tons of molten iron. Massive 500-ton capacity BOF cranes whose inch and one half diameter lifting cables, if unraveled, would stretch two miles. Looking through darkened goggles, you could peer into the interiors of cavernous furnaces reaching thousands of degrees, eliciting Dante's visions of Hell. There were giant press forges compressing two hundred ton orange-hot ingots into various shapes for machining. Massive ore bridge cranes, moving thirty tons of ore in each gaping mouthful of their huge buckets. Impressive oxygen furnaces, rotating to empty their bellies of hundreds of tons of molten steel into ladle cars with the capacities of Olympic swimming pools.

Thrown into the mix of all these prodigious industrial actions were a myriad of warning signs, flashing lights, whistles and sirens. Placards warning you of every possible hazard one could imagine: hazardous materials, radioactive materials, combustible materials, explosive materials, corrosive materials, lead hazards, asbestos hazards, noise hazards. If it was hazardous to your health or safety, it existed within the borders of Bethlehem Steel. Yet, with all of these perils, every day thousands of brave men and women would pass through the gates in an effort to give their families a more desirable life or give their children an opportunity to go to college.

So, at the worldly age of twenty, and of my own free will, on 11 December 1972, I enlisted in this industrial fraternity. I was issued a brass identification disc, or "check" which was about two inches in diameter to show to the guard upon entry to the plant. On the front were engraved the numbers 613-170. The first three digits indicated the shop you were assigned to. In this case the 613 indicated that it was the Saucon Division, Grey Mills, 42 inch rolling mill. The second set of three digits, 170, was my employee number. So, for the two years I spent on the "42", to the company clerks I was 170. To my buddies on the mill I was Neffy. To the older guys I was "that crazy kid" or "Spiderman" for my penchant for climbing anything on the mill. To me, I was a young guy looking at a bright future and about to make a fabulous income. My previous year I had earned $2,800, and currently had $7.00 in my checking account. My first full year as a steelworker I was to earn over $11,000. Now I was living the dream!

8 UNION MAN

Anyone seeking employment with Bethlehem Steel within the plant was informed that because it was a "closed shop", they were required to join the Union. Some new employees balked at this. I, however, had no problem with this, having a father who was a union man for most of his life. In fact, I was proud to become a member of the United Steel Workers of America, Local 2598. Being such a large company with an enormous workforce, the USWA had created three locals: 2598, 2599, and 2600.

In 1959, at the age of seven, I along with my parents and five brothers and sisters had suffered through the six-month strike at Bethlehem Steel. Occurring over fifty years ago, my recollections of that time are sparse. Some memories do stand out, however. Not knowing how long the strike would last, but expecting a long battle, my father gathered up myself and my brothers and headed off to our barber. The routine was simple. Leonard, our barber, would produce his giant comb-like apparatus, lay it on top of your head, and run an electric clippers over it, producing the ever-stylish "flat top". Twenty seconds.....twenty five cents. Even at seven years old I realized that people spent more time grooming their dogs, but Leonard did have a great pile of comic books.

This time would be different, though. With a quick movement of running his hand over his head, my father made his intentions understood. Leonard nodded and laid down his comb. Crew cuts for everyone. Haircut money had just been eliminated from the family budget. Three or four passes of the clippers over my tiny noggin and my auburn locks fell to the floor. A small donation to the union cause. My sisters fared better and were allowed to retain their tresses.

Food became an issue about three weeks into the strike. A typical lunch became a few crackers and a glass of milk. Supper became the ever-present bowl of potato soup. My mother became a magician at feeding her six children on an ever-decreasing food budget. The unions opened up a food bank, and to members with children it became a godsend. Baskets of potatoes were cheap and became a staple food for steelworker families.

I quickly became an arch enemy of potato soup. My mother tried many tactics to get me to eat it. The basic ruse of "Eat your soup, there are starving children in China" failed to move me. She even tried telling me that potato soup is considered a delicacy in France. "That figures," I thought. Only the French could liquefy a potato and try to sell it to Americans as fine cuisine. "Damn the French!"

Then my productive little mind came up with another tactic. With all the ardent fervor of a medieval alchemist, I tried to reconstitute the soup back into a potato. Crushed saltines and copious amounts of salt almost succeeded, but all it really did was turn it into potato mud. Failing as a chemist, I resigned myself to drinking it as fast as I could.

Within a few weeks the strike was over, and I saw the last of the potato soup. I never ate potato soup again. In 2011, however, while undergoing an upper GI test, I was asked to swallow a concoction with the consistency of thick potato mud. Had some pharmaceutical company waited fifty years to steal my invention? Or was it just cosmic payback?

Many people failed to see, and only a few realized what the steel strike achieved. The struggles of the union members at Bethlehem Steel, Mack Trucks, and Western Electric had a beneficial effect on all jobs in the Lehigh Valley. When benefits and wages rose for union members, owners of smaller companies had to raise their non-union employee wages and benefits for fear of losing their employees to the unions of the larger companies. I have never regretted one day of being a USWA member.

9 THE 42" MILL (RATS)

The Bethlehem Steel plant in South Bethlehem was immense, stretching from New Street on its west end to the border of Hellertown at its furthest eastern point, and running to the northeast along Applebutter Road. It was split into four divisions: Lehigh, Saucon, Coke Works, and East Lehigh.

The forty-two inch mill, where I was assigned, was the southern-most of the four operational rolling mills in the Saucon Division. Its designation was given to it because 42 inches was the widest structural I Beam it could roll. Adjacent to the north was the 48" Mill, then the 40 #1 Mill and then the northern-most mill, one quarter mile from the Lehigh River, the Combination Mill. Two rolling mills, the 28" Mill and the 12&18" Mill, had become obsolete when the Combination Mill was built, though they still stood, unused and derelict.

In December of 1972, the 42" mill was only rolling product on one shift or "turn" as it was called in the plant. That turn was 7 AM to 3 PM. I was hired to work as a scaleman on a clean-up shift which was from 3 PM to 11 PM. I mistakenly thought the scaleman's job was to weigh things. Being a scaleman was the lowest job on the Mill. When a steel ingot is shaped down to form a structural beam, as it is formed and cooled it develops a scaly outer coating. This coating is shed during the rolling process and collects under the roller line. My job was to spend four to six hours under the mills shoveling out the scale and grease. On the wall at the top of the stairs leading down to the netherworld, someone had scrawled the word "Hell" with an arrow pointing the way.

One was never alone in the subterranean chamber under the Mill while shoveling scale. There was a cable drag running the length of the roller line between the mills. Operating the drag would pull the loose scale toward the clean-out pit. Unfortunately, that wasn't all it would pull in. Discarded lunches or other edible refuse thrown between the rolls on the roller line by mill men too lazy to walk to a garbage can were also dragged in. When you operated the drag it was akin to ringing the dinner bell. Every rat within half a mile would come to dine and they were not timid in the least. The first time that I was "in the hole", when the rats appeared I headed up the stairway in haste. After getting used to this nightly culinary ritual, I would stand back and light up a cigarette. It was almost as though the few that would actually bump into you or run over your boot would look back at you with a "pardon me" gaze. We eventually came to an understanding. They would stay out of sight until we ran the drag. Then we would head up the stairs for lunch and leave them at their buffet in peace.

Later on, when I had advanced to the position of "table operator" at the #2 mill, one night shift about 3 AM I was sitting in the pulpit smoking, and looking back up the line toward the #1 mill. We were on about an hour of downtime, having no hot ingots to roll. About halfway between the mills some kind-hearted maintenance man had put out a bowl of milk and some dry cat food for one of the mill cats. "Cat" is a polite word used to describe these creatures. They had more of a resemblance to mangy gargoyles. It was rare to sight one. Sometimes they perched on the pulpit roofs to catch the heat from passing hot steel.

I was thinking how cold and utterly depressing it must be for any animal to live here when one appeared, evidently tempted by the saucer of milk. He looked cautiously around and proceeded to lap up his gift. Suddenly, in the blink of an eye, he ran off. A few moments later I realized why. Out from under the roller line sauntered a large rat. It was so large, it looked more like a dachshund wearing a Halloween rat mask.

I woke my buddy Hank up. He was sleeping on a bench at

the back of the pulpit. When his eyes finally focused, he saw it. I thought, "Great, I'm not hallucinating." He said, "What the fuck is that? It's as big as a fucking Volkswagen." Just then the mill whistle blew two times, meaning "Back to work, boys." A short time later I walked over to the milk bowl. I conservatively estimated, from the marks on the ground, that the rat was about 24" from nose to tail. Not exactly a VW, but big enough to make you cross to the other side of the street.

For many years, the steel industry had supported my family and thousands of other families in the Bethlehem area. But, known only to a few workers, there was a whole other stratum of life which relied on Bethlehem Steel for its survival. One wonders where the diminutive denizens of the Steel underworld vanished to, after the plant shut down and the free lunch disappeared.

10 CLOSE TO DEATH #1

I don't suppose many people wake up in the morning believing that they will die or come very close to death at their workplace. In my thirty years at Bethlehem Steel I came inches away from the grim reaper's scythe seven times.

My indoctrination into the "Halfway to Hell" club happened on a cold January Tuesday morning in 1973. Although rolling out beams with temperatures in the hundreds of degrees, the mill was a very cold place in the winter. The buildings housing the mills had open air roof monitors to facilitate smoke removal, and large doorway openings for the narrow gauge engines to enter, making them into virtual wind tunnels. My job that particular day was being a greaser. It wasn't a very strenuous job and had a lot of down time for smoking cigarettes and reading. You oiled and greased several places on the supplementary mill and main mill, and made sure the automatic grease pumps were functioning, keeping everything running smoothly. That took about fifteen minutes of the start of your shift. You did that twice in a shift and spent the rest of the time trying to amuse yourself.

I was just finishing oiling the main mill when I heard someone above me whistle. I looked up and "Wild Bill" Glauda, the number 2 Mill crane man, asked me if I wanted him to put the shed up on the platform. The shed was a three-sided structure with a roof and a bench. It was about six feet tall, eight feet wide, with a bench running the length of it. It was placed on the mill platform about fifteen feet from the roller line where the bars exited the #2 main mill, heading down to the hot saw where they would be cut to specs. The intended effect of the shed was to reflect the heat from the hot beams to warm its occupants.

The crane man lowered the shed into place. I unhooked the cables and waved my thanks to him. I then nestled into a corner of it, appreciating the warmth of the rolling steel going by. Having nothing to read, I lit up a Marlboro Light and just kicked back, waiting for someone in the roller shanty to come up and tell me the coffee was ready, or for the engineer working in a raised pulpit directly across the roller line from me to give me the coffee signal by tipping his hand up to his mouth.

To understand what happened next, I must explain what a "cobble" is.

It is desirable in the rolling and shaping of hot steel into H beams or I beams, for the orange, hot beams to behave and lay flat on the roller lines while being shaped. Occasionally and usually quite rarely a beam seems to be possessed by some demonic force. At the #2 mill on the 42" mill line, the supplementary mill lies in front of the main mill. Its job is to guide the hot beam into the main mill which then shapes and finishes the steel into the final product after several passes back and forth. If for any reason the main mill will not accept the beam, the leading end of the beam stops while the supplementary keeps pushing. This produces what is called a "cobble." The beam buckles in the twenty foot space between the mills, ending up looking like a two-ton piece of ribbon candy. A more deadly sister to a mid-mill cobble is the beam which exits the main mill and decides to go its own way. It may rise up like a cobra or hook left or right. When the engineer who guides the speed of the shaping mill sees a "snake", he scrams the mill, shutting it down. The beam usually travels thirty or forty feet before it stops.

So, this is what happened to me. Understanding this, the story takes an unexpected path into the supernatural realm. As I crushed out my last cigarette, I retreated to the far corner of the shed. After feeling the warmth of the rolling steel and listening to the rhythmic thumping of it exiting the Mill, I was lulled into a relaxing drowsiness. I really don't know how long I was asleep, but I woke to the overwhelming smell of freshly brewed coffee. Feeling a good dose of caffeine was exactly what I needed to wake up, I rose, left the shed, turned right, went down the three steps of the mill platform, and walked over to the roller shanty.

As I opened the door, I heard a very loud crash. I turned and saw the shed I had just left lifted up and thrown into the hand railing around the mill platform. The engineer had shut down the mill as soon as the beam snaked. Now, the entire mill back up the line shut down, waiting for millwrights with cutting torches to cut up the cobble. In the meantime, everyone on the mill assembled at the #2 mill. The engineer named Steiny walked over to me, white faced, and said, "Sweet Christ, Neffy, what the fuck made you get up and leave twenty seconds before that beam hit the exact spot you were sitting in?"

"I smelled coffee!!" I replied.

Big Bill Green, the roller, looked at me and said, "We didn't make the coffee yet."

As I looked at Steiny, I finally realized what had just happened and felt weak in the knees. Seeing my reaction, Big Bill grabbed my arm and walked me over to the steps, up to the platform, and said "Get up there kid!"

"Why?" I asked.

"If you don't go up now, you'll never go back up there."

I heeded his advice and returned and helped clean up the mess. Even though they moved the shed adjacent to the mill to prevent any other employees getting speared by a hot beamI never sat in it again. I purchased new long underwear and wore a double set. A heartfelt "thank you" went to my guardian angel who brewed the coffee. I started with nine lives and I had just used one up. Little did I know that before my Bethlehem Steel career was over I would use up six more, and my guardian angel would be working overtime.

11 INTO A PULPIT

It was only a few weeks later that my seniority landed me a learner's position on the mill. Finally, out of the grease and into a pulpit! A pulpit was an elevated working platform surrounded by large sheets of glass, protecting the operators from the heat and noise of the mill. I was training to learn the "supplementary mill operators" job in the #2 pulpit on the mill. Under the tutelage of Hank "The Battler" Sadawski, I learned the job rather quickly. It wasn't rocket science, but it did take coordination. We had a very talented and effective group of guys in the pulpits. "Cowboy" (I never really knew his real name), was the "bloomer operator." The "Shearman" was Jimmy Donchez. The #1 shaping mill was operated by Rick Serman and Jim Horn. The #2 Mill was Hank and Sam Bissey.

When the 42 had gone to two shifts, I had been placed on the second shift where many of the workers were my age. Most of the older workers had gone to first shift because they liked working day shift. The younger crew on the second shift liked to joke around and play practical jokes on each other. All the guys would go out together after work, forming a bond with each other over our beers and boiler makers at local places like the Smugglers, the Lehigh Tavern, the Tally Ho, and Tammany Hall.

The job I was learning was operating the roller lines on either side of the mill and raising and lowering the rolls of the supplementary mill. Sam was the "Screwdown operator". His job was the final shaping of the beam by raising and lowering the main rolls and the side rolls. Rick would send the bar down the line from #1 and I would send it into the supplementary mill and stop it on the other side of the main mill by reversing the rollerline and stopping the bar. It would make two or three passes into the #2 mill before it was finished. On the final pass I would send it down the roller line about three hundred feet where the "hot saw" operator would pull it over onto his roller line and feed it into the saw. If everyone did their job, it really was effective at pushing out tons of structural steel.

One bright sunny day, about halfway through our shift, I was bringing a bar down from #1. Hank is sitting next to me observing, and Sam is five feet away, chewing tobacco and operating the screw down controls. Just as Sam put in a new wad of "chew" and spit in a bucket in the back corner of the pulpit, Hank bursts out laughing. As I look out the window, there is Cowboy, on a break from his bloomer job, standing out on the platform. He's eating a jar of octopus. With two long tentacles hanging out of his mouth, he comes up to the pulpit window. Sam, who can't see what we're laughing at, cranes his head and sees Cowboy, who is now slowly sucking in the tentacles. He swallows his chewing tobacco and begins to vomit all over his controls. Hank is on the floor laughing, I have a bar going through the mill and I'm about to lose my lunch from the smell, and Cowboy is running back up the line to his job. We managed to stop the bar without killing anyone, shut down the mill, and hosed out the pulpit. Sam went home sick and the turn foreman came over and asked what happened. Nobody said anything. Just another day on the 42. God I love this job!

12 HAMMERIN' HANK SADAWSKI

If your fellow millworkers liked you, they hung a nickname on you. If they didn't like you......you didn't get one. It was an industrial badge of honor to acquire one. Over the years I acquired many: Neffy, Spiderman, Noodles, and Nunzio among them.

It was during the latter phase of my table operator training that I came to realize how my buddy Hank "The Battler" Sadawski had acquired his rather menacing moniker. After two weeks of training, I had become quite at ease with the task of bringing a hot bar down the roller line from the number one mill, into the supplementary mill, through the main mill, and stopping it on the other side, waiting and then returning it back through the mill. This procedure happened two or three times, depending on what size beam it was to become.

Hank and I had struck up a friendship when I started my training. He always had a pack of Marlboro Lights lying on the control console and I would help myself to a smoke now and then. I knew I was smoking too many when Hank told me he was going to claim me as a dependent when tax season rolled around. He was placated when an anonymous donor placed two cartons of Marlboros in his locker.

On one shift, things were going smoothly. I was the table operator. Hank was behind me, observing my progress. And an acerbic guy named Ray was the screwdown operator. Ray was usually tolerable but had a tendency toward practical jokes.

As a table operator, one of your jobs was to raise and lower the upper and lower rolls of the Supplementary Mill. The control for this was a lever operating a rotating drum with marks on it. You would "hit" your mark and run the bar through on the first shaping pass. Then you would raise and lower the rolls on the return pass where the bar ran freely. Then you hit your mark for the second shaping pass and feed your bar into the mill. Once you were adept at this procedure, it became rather monotonous but you had the knowledge to correct, if anything went awry.

We're about three hours into our shift. I have a bar going through the mill and I'm watching the monitor to view when it comes out on the other side. Now Ray decides to have some fun with the new trainee and test his skills. He leans over and slaps the lever on my control panel, sending the drum spinning. Hank, seated behind me, gets up and calmly says "Neffy, stay with the bar," and moves the control lever, spinning the drum back to its mark. He looks at Ray and says "Don't do that."

The next bar coming down, third pass, Ray slaps the lever. I was astute enough to recover and Hank says "Good job, Neffy," followed by "Ray, don't do that again."

The next bar coming down, Ray leans over and slaps the lever. Before he took his hand off the lever, Hank lands a punch on the side of Ray's head, knocking him off of his chair. Now it becomes a steel cage wrestling match in an 8' X 8' pulpit. While they're crashing around, I somehow manage to stop the bar after its final pass, and grab the intercom phone.

As I'm screaming at Rick, working at the #1 Mill, to stop the bar he's sending down, Hank and Ray are still swinging and punching. They tumble out of the pulpit door, down three steps and onto the roller-line platform. Fortunately Rick sees the fight going on at Number 2 in his pulpit mirror and stops the bar he's sending down. I grab the intercom mike and call for the roller, Joe Temlin.

"What's going on, Neffy?" he answered.

"Hank and Ray are fighting!"

"They're always fighting, let them alone," Joe said.

I scream back, "Not arguing! Hank has Ray's head on the fucking roller line and he's choking him! Get the fuck over here!"

Joe comes running over with some of the guys from the build-up gang and break them up. Still sweating and bleeding, Hank and Ray get up, shake hands, and climb back up into the pulpit.

The next bar comes rolling down from Number One Mill and I send it into the mill. While we're running it through on its first pass, I look over at Hank and Ray and say, "Could you guys do that again? I missed most of it when you knocked me off my fuckin' chair." They bust out laughing. I bum another smoke from Hank, light up and lean back in my chair.

"Just another day on the 42. I love this fuckin' job."

13 FIRST BLOOD

In my last year of employment with Bethlehem Steel I happened to be in the company's medical dispensary one day and on a whim asked to see my medical records. Whenever a steelworker had to visit the dispensary, the staff filled in a form which hopefully included a "release to work". You got a copy, and the medical department held the original in your file. What the nurse handed me was a collection of thirty years of slips, thicker than a Manhattan telephone directory. She looked at the packet she was holding, then looked at me and said, "How did you survive all this?"

"Prayers, exercise, and megavitamins."

Although my time working on the 42 was a mere eighteen months of the thirty years I spent working for Bethlehem Steel, looking back, it was a good and relatively safe place to begin one's career. I'm not saying the 42 was without danger. My first major bloodletting misfortune happened there, only six months into my industrial career. We were working middle shift (3 PM – 11 PM) and I was working up on the Number 2 Mill platform. I was returning from the hot saw, sent there by the Roller "Big Bill" Green, to pick up a sample of the bars we were rolling.

This was a common practice. The roller would signal the second guide setter by holding his hand up, with his thumb and index finger pinched together. The second guide setter would walk the three hundred feet down the line and make the same hand gesture to the hot saw operator sitting twenty feet up in her pulpit. Seeing the signal, the saw operator would cut a two inch piece off the beam. I would then cool it off in a water trough, and hammer down the flange edges.

After acquiring a test sample, I headed back to the roller shanty by crossing over the cooling bed, which meant stepping over a few constantly moving orange-hot twelve hundred degree bars. Having run this gauntlet, I was home free and strolling up to the door with the section sample in my right hand, reaching for the door handle with my left. This is when I slipped on a pool of grease. I fell forward, my left hand extended, and it went right through the glass window pane. That's not what injured me. It was abruptly pulling my hand back which lacerated my wrist. A razor sharp, jagged piece of glass laid my wrist open about 2 ½ inches.

Big Bill came out, looked at me, and said "What did you do now, son?" Looking at my arm he said, "That's a bad one. Head up to the dispensary right now."

"But Bill, I don't know where it is," I replied.

Looking around, Bill says "Joe, walk the kid up to the dispensary." After an uneventful twenty-minute walk up and down stairs and through an eight foot concrete tunnel about one quarter mile long under railroad tracks, we arrived.

At this time the Company had a dispensary at the Lehigh and Saucon Divisions. The nurse, looking up at me when I entered, seemed a bit put out. "What's your Department and number," she asked. Not being used to working for a company where you're just a number, I replied "Larry Neff."

"Number, please?" she barked.

"Well," I thought, "I'm not bleeding to death, let's have some fun."

With a more authoritative tone she says, "What is your injury?"

"I fell through a window," I answered.

"How the hell did you manage to do that," she asked.

"Slipped on grease," I said.

"What did you injure," she asked in a more empathetic tone.

"I have a 2 ½' laceration on my wrist," I answered.

"Right or left?" she asked.

"Left."

"Left wrist laceration. Is that correct?"

"That's right," I said.

"Oh, it's your right wrist. Sorry about that," she said, erasing the form.

"No! It's my left wrist," I corrected her.

"Left wrist injury, right?"

"Right," I said through a half smile. I could see in her eyes that she knew she was being played. She puts down her pencil, takes off her reading glasses, looks at me, and says "Who's on first?" I burst out laughing and replied "Who is." She smiles and says "OK, Mr. Neff, let's get that arm cleaned up."

After a rigorous cleaning, the doctor, who was called in from home and not too amused about it, sewed me up with eight rather nice stitches. Walking back down the tunnel to the 42, reading my first dispensary "released to work" slip, I thought to myself "Now, I'm a steelworker."

14 SHOP TALK

One night in the spring of '73, I was working a three-to-eleven shift. I was still in training on the Number Two mill, table operator position. We had "blown down" the mill for "nothing hot." This simply meant that we had no hot ingots to roll. Occasionally Cowboy, the bloomer operator, would get bored and fidgety and blow a short blast on the bloomer whistle, signaling the pit crane operator to put a hot ingot into the transfer buggy. A single calm voice would come over the mill intercom: "Nothing hot."

Down time meant you were free to do whatever you wanted to do. Rick Serman, who was the screwdown operator, was leaning back in his chair reading a magazine. Hank, who was training me, was half asleep on a bench. I was sitting in the table operators' seat smoking and listening to the radio. I had recently bought an aerial from Radio Shack, climbed up the building columns, and installed it on the 42 roof. Then I had run a cable behind the crane run and wired it into our radio. We had gone from listening to static-suffocated local stations to clear stations from Philadelphia and New York.

After hearing Cowboys' tenth or eleventh hoot from his bloomer whistle, a rather stressed voice came over the intercom. "Cowboy, we will call you when the ingots are hot enough to roll.....If I hear that whistle once more, I'll come over there and shove your head so far up your ass, you can eat your breakfast all over again."

As hoots and jeers came over the intercom, I heard Hank waking up in the corner. He looks up at me and says, "Do you know who that was on the intercom, talking to Cowboy?"

"No,"

"It was your father!"

"Bullshit! My father doesn't talk like that." I look at Rick and he's grinning and nodding his head up and down. "Can't be. My Dad is a pit recorder on the 40 #1 pits."

"We're getting our steel from the 40 #1 tonight," Hank said. "One of the 42 pit cranes is fucked up and down for repairs."

"But I've lived with him for twenty years!" I protested. "I never heard him talk like that."

Hank got up, pulled a cigarette from the pack, lit up and said, "We all do that. Talking in here is different than on the outside. It's called "shop talk". The only time I talk like we do in here on the outside, it's to my ex-wife."

Rick and I broke up. "Well, I suppose I'll find out at eleven. I rode to work with my Dad," I said.

On the half-mile walk to the parking lot, I said "Hey, I heard you on the mill intercom tonight."

He looked sideways at me and said, "It's the only type of language some of these idiots understand."

"Well, at least you shut Cowboy up."

"Cowboy can be a fucking asshole sometimes," he replied. This was the first time my father had ever spoken to me as a union brother, not a son. As I slipped into the passenger seat of his Plymouth, he looked at me and said "Don't talk like that around your mother."

On the way home, I looked at my reflection in the window and thought, "**Now** I'm a fucking steelworker!"

15 BECOMING A RIGGER

I was laid off from the 42" mill in December of 1974. In March of '75 I decided, since my unemployment checks were running out, that I should seek out another job within the plant. After having been unemployed for several months, my habitual rising time of 5:30 AM had changed to 10:00 AM, giving me just enough time to throw on some clothes, jump in my MGB, and drive to McDonalds for a coffee and two Egg McMuffins before they started serving lunch. I would then head down to check the Steel employment office's "jobs available" board which was just inside the main gate. On a sunny April morning I checked the board and found a posting for six rigger apprentices. For a moment I pondered "What the hell is a rigger" but then I had a flashback to a night working on the 42.

We had just finished up on a roll change at the number 2 mill and were taking a smoke break on the mill platform when a group of guys wearing battleship gray helmets came walking down the mill line.

"Who are those guys?" I asked, pointing to them.

"They're riggers. Toughest fuckers in the plant." Just then one of the riggers recognized Hank and came over to talk to him. "Hi, Roy," Hank said. "What the fuck are you guys doing down here?"

"We're here to prep for a crane rail change," Roy said.

Pointing to me, Hank said "This is the guy you want working

with you. He climbs everything around here like a monkey." That was true enough: my love of climbing had only grown. Mill stands, roll racks or building columns would placate me until the weekends, when sheer rock walls were my desire. Stretching his hand out to shake, Roy said "Glad to meet you. We could use you if you like to climb."

"Would love it," I said.

Hank cut in. "He also has another talent that would make him fit right in with you guys."

"What's that?"

"He can pick locks!"

Roy grinned and said "You'd be a tremendous asset to the department!"

Afterward the conversation had stayed in the back of my mind. A chance to climb for a living? Sounded like fun.

In reality, one of my nicknames, "Spiderman", wasn't conferred upon me by my mill brothers, but by an eight-year-old boy from West Bethlehem. In the advent of my climbing career, I would hang out with my friends at the basketball court on the Calypso School playground in West Bethlehem. The school building adjacent the court had wire mesh screens over the windows to protect the glass. Inevitably, children throwing or hitting tennis balls would find them stuck in the screens.

One sunny autumn day while we were playing basketball, a small boy asked us if we could retrieve his tennis ball, stuck in a third floor screen. Any climber worth his salt would consider this a challenge: a "free" climb using no technical gear or ropes. Any rational person would consider this an invitation to an ambulance ride. Taking the irrational approach of "no risk.....no glory", I free climbed the sturdy rain downspout, traversed the third floor window ledges using the shaky screens as handholds, and rescued the ball.

Reversing my course, I descended fully intact. I was approached by the boy and his mother.

"Go ahead," she said to him.

"Thank you, Mr. Spiderman," he sheepishly replied.

His mother laughed and told me, "When you were up there, stuck to the wall, he said you looked like Spiderman." I smiled and thanked them. Walking back to the basketball game, I was hit with a plethora of good-natured jeering from my buddies.

Of all my climbing, I will always remember it as one of my best free climbs. It wasn't a 5-10 or Everest. But then, what idiot would climb Mount Everest to retrieve a tennis ball?

After recalling that memory of my first meeting, I felt that my choice of signing up to join the riggers was the correct one. In retrospect, after thirty years of blood, sweat, and tears, I still believe that.

My apprenticeship as a rigger began in May and was designed to be a four year course. You went out every day with a rigger gang and put in eight hours learning the particulars of each job. Since most of the jobs to which we were assigned were extremely dangerous, the apprenticeship became more like a survival course.

You were tested as you learned: operating a burning torch, climbing, 28 different rope knots and their uses, rigging up air hoists, and walking steel high in the air (if you fell, you failed.) The riggers operated under the working theory that any fall over fourteen feet was a lethal fall, because that gave you enough time to spin mid-air and land on your head. It therefore made no difference if you were working at fifteen feet or fifty feet. The point was moot, because we were usually working two hundred to three hundred feet in the air.

The only respite from this tough schedule was every other Tuesday. That is when you went to apprentice class, in a classroom on the second floor of the electrical shop. The class consisted of about twenty pupils from various departments. Riggers, pipefitters, carpenters, electricians and machinists made up the class. All of the classes were ICS (International Correspondence Courses) courses. As riggers, we were issued a rigger training manual which had a copyright date of 1932. The book hadn't changed a bit since then and the tests that were given bi-weekly had been the same for over forty years. Chester Frankenfield was a rigger who had taken the same course in 1936, and had the foresight to save copies of all the right answers. I had worked with Chester for about a year and had learned many things from him until he retired. His folder of well-thumbed pages with the correct answers had helped many riggers pass their courses. Never being one to break from such a long and coveted tradition, I dutifully copied down the answers to my tests and was deemed by my ICS instructors to be an excellent student.

Tuesdays in rigger apprentice school were long. Frequent coffee breaks and cigarette breaks were interspersed with cat naps and perusing the eight-foot high stack of Playboys and Penthouse magazines. After a few months of this, I began stopping on Mondays after work at the Bethlehem Public Library and checking out books to read at school. Who could have known that one of those pretty research librarians who helped me choose books would, thirty five years later, become my partner, lover and friend.

16 THE VOICE FROM BEYOND

About six months into the apprenticeship we got our first chance to work on a large-scale job. It was a total rebuild of Blast Furnace E. E was the eastern-most furnace of the five remaining furnaces. A rebuild was a massive undertaking requiring most of the rigger force, about 130, plus numerous other crafts all working side by side.

At the start of the rebuild we would assist PA (public address) servicemen to install a loud speaker communications system over the entire furnace. There were about twenty speakers bolted to columns on the cast floor, charging floor, bell lever platform, superstructure, and as high up as the bleeder platform, which is the top of the furnace. All of the speakers were aimed to face downward.

About three or four days into our new job we were scheduled on an 8 PM to 8 AM twelve-hour shift. Having a choice, most of us working night shift would have preferred working day shift. But being the low men on the seniority list, we worked it without complaint. The job had started in mid-October and it was an exceptionally clear and cold night around midnight when we stopped for a lunch break.

I believe the idea came to us while we were standing on the charging floor, about 150' up on the furnace facing out toward the Lehigh River. While I was standing there with Jeff Gehringer, Bruce Ward, and Tom OHaire, Jeff pointed across the river to a building and asked what it was.

"That's a high rise apartment building for senior citizens."

I believe it was Bruce who said, "I wonder if they could hear Nick over there." We all started laughing. Nicky was an A Rigger, or gang leader. His job that night was signal man. He was responsible for the coordinated lifting of heavy objects from the cast floor to the men working high up on the furnace. Needless to say, he was the main voice on the twenty or so loudspeakers.

It was no problem to us that he used rather colorful language. I would admit that anyone working on the furnace that night wasn't entirely free of using the work "fuck" in some form, interspersed throughout their conversation. Nick, however, had taken it to a completely different level. Had he devoted that energy to music, he would have been another Bach or Brahms; if to art, another Van Gogh or Monet. But I suppose he was content with being a spinner of expletives.

I really don't remember whose idea it was, but it was brilliant. Armed with only adjustable wrenches, the four of us climbed the entire furnace, readjusting all of the loudspeakers so they were aimed north across the river. It was dangerous enough walking steel during daylight hours, but much more walking it in the dark. It was well worth the effort though. We didn't know it at the time, but our stunt would go down in rigger history. We managed to get back in time to gobble down a sandwich and coffee when the men from other gangs started stumbling back, half asleep from their lunch hour. No one noticed or even cared why the four of us were soaked with sweat. We just went back to work and soon the lifting began and Nicky sang his sweet song.

At about 3:30 in the morning, someone noticed that lights in the high rise and houses along Church St. began blinking on. About 4:00 AM a new voice came over the PA system. It was rigger foreman Ed Leiby: "Everyone working on this furnace report to the cast floor immediately!"

It took about twenty minutes for the sixty riggers, pipefitters, carpenters, and electricians to assemble. While everyone is milling around wondering what the fuck was going on, someone sees a plant patrol vehicle coming to a stop on the service road.

"What the fuck is going on, Ed?" remarked one of the pipefitters.

"If the plant patrol broke up their pinochle game to come over here at 4 AM, somebody must have fuckin' died!" Everyone laughed.

Just about then two plant patrol officers escorting two Bethlehem police officers climbed the stairs and came onto the cast floor. The Bethlehem officers stood there in their spotless uniforms and shined shoes looking at sixty tough sons of bitches, dirty from head to toe, smoking cigarettes or spitting chewing tobacco. It wouldn't have been much different if these officers were touring a Soviet gulag. They stood there realizing that they were getting a glimpse of a steel mill that few people do.

Ed Leiby turned out to be a gracious host, giving a quick tour, but then someone asked Ed if there was going to be coffee and cake after the tour. Ed was a tough rigger before becoming a foreman, so he simply answered with a "Fuck you guys" and laughed.

Bringing the two officers over to stand before our group, he introduced them. "These gentlemen would like to have a word with you. Go ahead, officers."

The younger officer spoke first. "Guys, we're getting a lot of calls about profanity and cursing coming across the river from your loudspeakers."

Nick, standing in the front of the group, looks at the officer and says "Who the fuck was cursing?" Everyone lost it. Just about then I see Ed looking up at the loudspeakers. Now he's looking at us. I looked at Jeff and Bruce. "We're fucked. He knows."

Ed tells the officers he understands what's going on. After having a ride up the small claustrophobic elevator to the charging floor for a lovely view of the sleeping city, the police left. Ed motions to me, Jeff and Bruce to come over to him.

"New job, guys," he said. "The three of you will climb this fucking furnace and aim all of those speakers down and I don't care if you have to hang by your fuckin balls to do it!"

We finished when the sun was coming up. In my thirty years at Bethlehem Steel, that was the only time I had ever seen Bethlehem police officers in the plant, and it took the riggers to do it

17 THE BUCKET DROP

It wasn't long after I joined the Riggers that I learned it was a department that was frequently given jobs that other departments shied away from, and on many occasions simply refused to do. They would claim the jobs were impossible or insane to attempt. This is where the Rigger Department earned its reputation.

In many instances, jobs had plans to go by and safety rules to adhere to. Riggers were trained in many of the same disciplines that millwrights and repairmen were. We excelled, however, at one thing which differentiated us from all of the other departments. We never followed the rules. The more extreme an assignment, the more Riggers wanted to do it. It could be said that we suffered from inflated egos, but I believe it was more like living up to the reputation that had been built over many years by the riggers that had gone before us. We frequently pulled off stunts that, had we been in another department, we would have been severely disciplined or terminated for even thinking about. Our reputation also afforded us a certain "untouchability."

After a brutally hot and miserable repair shift at the sintering plant, located on the north side of the Minsi Trail Bridge, the forty or so riggers working that job got in the habit of retiring to a row of garages directly beneath the bridge. Waiting an hour or so for the bus to take us back to the rigger building, we would sit around smoking and talking or a pinochle game would begin. On one shift,

Bob Solt, one of the younger riggers and a former Marine, developed an extreme game. It was sort of a "chicken" game. We would climb up a ladder onto a 36" gas line which ran the length of the bridge about six feet beneath. Two men would stand on the pipe and put their fingers through the open grating of the bridge roadway and grip it. You then had to listen for an approaching car and at the last second pull your fingers out. Over the years it was played several times and no one ever lost any fingers. Either we developed the reflexes of mongooses or we were just incredibly lucky.

One time, on a beautiful crisp October day an event transpired that would test our untouchable status. A new foreman, a "looper" and graduate of Lehigh University, had recently started working as a production foreman at the Sintering Plant. He became accustomed to parking his Volkswagen Beetle in a garage that we used for our pinochle games. He returned one day after a late lunch, and saw that we had returned the table to his private garage and were playing cards. After a few meaningful toots of his horn, he was politely encouraged by the assembled group to go fuck himself. Angered, he drove off to park somewhere else.

The following week we arrived after our repair shift to our pinochle garage to find our wooden table sitting atop the garage and the Volkswagen parked there. The looper was a bit misguided in believing that this was the end of it. I was amazed at the short amount of time it took my eight husky rigger brothers to pick up a VW, shuffle their feet in unison, turn the car and place it sideways in the garage. He pushed…..we pushed back. It was simply a matter of testosterone levels!

We were still sitting around when he came to retrieve his car. As he opened the doors, his reaction was wholly unexpected. He started laughing and said, "You fuckin guys play rough." In a few minutes, our ruffled feathers smoothed out, his car was rotated back to the correct position. Mutual respect was achieved.

We truly were not in the habit of following rules. One cold March day, three hundred feet in the air at the top of D furnace, ignoring a basic tenet of safety, Rigger Pete Chando and I took a ride I will never forget.

We were working a clean-up shift. The gigantic lattice boom mobile crane that we had been using for the past five months was in a fixed position situated at the north side of the furnace yard. The crane, operator and mechanic were from a rigging company out of Philadelphia, McHugh Rigging and Hauling. The two-man crew had worked with us for the past six months on a total rebuild of D Furnace. The area that the crane was positioned in made it impossible for him to see where we were working, so all lifting and dropping commands were done over handheld Motorola UHF radios. When working high on a furnace you have to be totally confident in your crane operator. He has to sit there with a headset and mike and move a thirty ton crane with a 350 foot boom gently to make the smallest adjustments on our end.

The operator we had worked with for most of the rebuild was the best. He was young but he possessed the skill and touch of an old timer. In the early days after the crane was in position and the 350 foot boom was erected, he had dropped his lifting hook to about fifteen feet from the ground and painted the lifting cable bright yellow where it came off the lifting drum to give himself a visual cue for when the load on the hook would be nearing the ground. Painting that cable was simply an extra safety precaution, which more likely than not saved two lives.

Pete and I were cleaning up scrap metal that was left over from a job on the gas bleeder platform, which is the highest point on any of the blast furnaces. During furnace operations, the bleeders would open at intervals to release excess pressure. The resulting large cloud of gas emanating from the furnace was mostly carbon monoxide. Any unfortunate pigeon flying through the emission cloud would take one or two breaths and drop like a rock from the sky. Most experienced employees working in any area adjacent to the furnace would cast a wary eye skyward after hearing the ear-piercing release of gas from the bleeders, expecting an occasional feathered bomb. A direct hit from a one pound pigeon falling from three hundred feet would tend to unravel your day.

Pete had just positioned a scrap box at a level even with the hand railing of the platform. The box, which was eight feet long by five feet wide and four feet deep, was attached to the crane hook by two eight foot long, one inch braided steel cables. When the box was loaded, Pete would radio the crane operator with very precise instructions to navigate the box between obstructions and get it to the drop point which was a straight drop to the ground. Once this location was reached and the load had stopped swinging, he would signal the crane operator to lower down the load. As the load started to lower, if the signal man said "Highball", the crane operator would drop the load at high speed.

There is a very strict OSHA rule that no one, at any time, for any reason, and under no possible circumstance may "ride the load". As riggers, we could always see the flexibility of this directive. After having thrown the last few remnants of scrap into the bucket, I lit up a cigarette and turned to Pete.

"It's almost lunch time." Pointing to the scrap bucket, I said "Why don't we take the elevator down?"

"Are you out of your fuckin mind? We can't do that!"

"No, we're not SUPPOSED to do that," I said. "Who the fuck will see us? Only the crane operator, when we land, and he won't say a fuckin word."

Climbing into the bucket, whose edge came up to our waists, we held onto the cables and began our illegal trip. Pete radioed the operator and we began floating through the air until we reached the drop point. We were now about three hundred feet in the air, looking down and admiring the view as the box stopped its swinging from side to side. I looked at Pete and said, "Just don't Highball," not knowing that he had just pressed the radio transmit button.

All the operator heard was "Highball".

For one moment as we dropped, we experienced zero gravity and were standing in mid-air. It was similar to what befell the coyote in most of the Road Runner cartoons. We quickly regained gravity and collapsed in the bucket. All I saw, looking up, was the top of the furnace receding from view and heard the whirring sound of the load cable.

Thank God the operator knew his limit marks. He stopped the box about ten feet above the ground and after it stopped bobbing up and down, he gently lowered it to the ground. I looked over at Pete and he grinned and said "What a fuckin rush."

As we popped up from the bottom of the box, the operator almost fell off his rig. He jumped down off of his crane and said, "I've worked with some crazy fuckin bastards before, but you guys just scored ten out of ten for that stunt."

"Relax, Eddie," I said. "We just didn't want to be late for lunch."

I don't believe Pete and I will ever get in the Guinness Book for the highest industrial freefall in a scrap box, but it's still a story told at Rigger reunions.

18 GREAT BALL OF FIRE

My next brush with catastrophic injury nearly had my guardian angel tearing up his time card while standing by the heavenly time clock. To my great relief he relented, and was there when I needed him the most.

As we walked to our next job, it seemed like just another day. The gang that day included Bob "Mosh" Holowka, (called "Johnny" by his rigger buddies), and "Fritz" Werner as the two welders. The A man, or leader of the gang, was Dennis Hoffman. I was the B man or burner in the crew. My expertise was in using a cutting torch.

It was a bitterly cold day in January of 1986 and even colder when you get assigned to work in the basement of the EFM (Electric Furnace Melting) department. Our job that day was to fabricate and weld supports into the floor beams supporting the furnace above us. With the temperature hovering around ten degrees and damp, we decided to try to warm the place up.

We noticed a very large pipe above us with spray painted stenciled letters saying "natural gas" and a convenient valve to attach a hose to. This pipe carried high pressured gas to the furnace above us. We didn't think the furnace men from EFM would mind if we siphoned off some gas to keep us warm.

There are quite a few ways to build a heating device to provide warmth. We used one of the simplest methods available to us that day. We attached a rubber hose to the gas line with a pipe fixed to the other end of the hose. We then took a discarded 35-gallon metal drum, burned a hole in the side, and filled it half way with a pile of furnace brick. The idea was to turn the pipe valve on, ignite the gas coming out of it, and put the pipe into the barrel where the brick would diffuse the flame.

Our little heater worked quite well for a time. Its only drawback, however, was that the pipe we were using to feed the heater was about eight feet long and we kept tripping on it. Dennis, lighting up the last Marlboro from his pack and tossing the pack into the barrel, motioned to me to come over.

"What's up?" I asked.

"Get your burning torch and cut about six feet off of this pipe so we don't keep tripping over it," he said.

"Give me a sec, I have two more stiffeners to cut out of that plate, and then I'll get to it," I replied. Finishing up my work a few minutes later, I pulled my burning torch and its hose over to the heater barrel. Turning the valve on the gas pipe to the off position, shutting off the gas flow, I pulled the pipe from the barrel and handed it to Dennis. He measured it and put a mark on it where he wanted it cut off.

This is probably the point in time where things started to go terribly wrong. This is also when my personal guardian angel (I truly believe we all have one) shook his head somberly from side to side and thought, "Oh God, not again."

I knelt down, positioned the pipe for cutting, lit my cutting torch with the striker hanging from a chain on my belt, slid the rubber burner goggles down from my hard hat over my eyes, and cut the pipe off. I picked up the pipe, which was now about three feet long, cracked open the valve slightly and walked toward the barrel. My intention was to put the pipe back into the barrel and then ignite the gas in the barrel with my cutting torch. I had been using my burning goggles to cut the pipe, and had forgotten to put my safety glasses back on. They remained tucked in the top pocket of my jacket. I proceeded to stick the pipe with natural gas flowing out of it into the hole in the side of the barrel.

What I was unaware of was that, being a high pressure line, the pipe was pumping gas out at a rapid pace. I was also unaware that Dennis' previously discarded Marlboro pack hadn't entirely burned up but was laying on the bricks in the barrel, smoldering. At the last second, my sense of smell made me aware of the fact that I was standing in a giant sphere of unignited natural gas. A moment later the gas reached the fire of the cigarette box.

It was only by the grace of God that I blinked my eyes when the Great Ball of Fire engulfed me. I still wince when I hear Jerry Lee Lewis pounding that song out. When it ignited, I heard a low "whoof" sound and felt a searing flash of heat, but only for a brief second. I remember reaching for the valve on the pipe and shutting the gas off. For a moment I had no vision and instinctively brought my hands up to my eyes. For a few unnerving moments I believed I had just lost my sight. I was a father with two young sons who relied on me, and I had just done something rather stupid and blinded myself.

The flame had hit me when I blinked and had melted my eyelashes together. I pried my eyelids apart, and was relieved to realize my eyesight was intact. I was also relieved to see Johnny, Dennis and Fritz all laughing at me. Most people would think of this as terribly insensitive, but to me it meant I wasn't badly injured. It was mainly a slight blow to my vanity. My eyelashes, eyebrows, and mustache were gone and my well-groomed full beard was substantially reduced. But I could see.

About this time our foreman Walter, showed up.

"What the fuck happened to you?" he asked.

"Fire barrel malfunction," I said.

"What are you going to tell the nurse at the medical center?"

"Well, when I walk in with all the hair burned off of my face, after they stop laughing, they'll slap some silvadene on my face and send me back," I said.

I suffered more from jokes and new nicknames I received over the next two weeks than I did from the actual burns. Mack McLaughlin hung the moniker of "Neffy the Human Torch" on me, but being a long-time fan of The Fantastic Four that didn't bother me all that much. After three or four weeks of looking like a human/alien hybrid, my eyebrows and eyelashes grew back and I set off seeking my next explosive or body altering adventure. Which, it turned out, was only a few weeks away.

19 THE POWER TOWER

My next test of survival, walking the razor's edge between life and death at Bethlehem Steel, came less than three weeks after healing from the aftereffects of my accidental two hundred degree natural gas hair removal treatment.

The day began, like a thousand other mornings, by walking into a small hole in the wall called Eddie's Diner (not in existence since 1992). The coffee was astonishingly good. Most of us, however, were somewhat cautious about the food being served. To most riggers, breakfast at Eddie's Diner was a coffee, a doughnut, and a cigarette. This meal evolved from simple logic. The coffee was great, the cigarettes were your own, and Eddie would have to go a very long way to fuck up a donut. As I walked in, my rigger buddy Willy D. Chain was seated at the last stool at the counter, smoking a cigarette and reading the newspaper. He turned and greeted me as I took the stool next to him.

"Morning, Neffy, how's it going?"

"Same old shit, different day, Willy."

"I knows what you mean, man." Willy had been born and raised in the Peach State and came to the Lehigh Valley looking for work when he was young. We called him "Willy D" because his name was Willy and he bore a remarkable resemblance to the actor Billy D. Williams. This, along with a few other traits, made him a chick magnet. In the thirty years I worked with him, he taught me many things. Although he worked most of his life in Pennsylvania, he always seemed to wish to go back to his home state of Georgia.

I sat down and lit up a smoke. The waitress came over to take my order. "Just a coffee, honey, and a donut," I said. She smiled, wrote down my order, turned and walked away. This is where our somewhat optimistic hope for a shining new day started going downhill.

The waitress brought a plate over and set it down in front of Willy. He folded up his newspaper and laid it on the counter, picked up a fork and started to dig into his eggs, home fries and bacon. A second later I looked over at him and he was sitting there motionless.

"What the fuck's wrong?" I asked. He turned to me and said "My bacon is movin' by itself." I spit my last sip of coffee out through my nose and started laughing. Willy took his fork and lifted up the bacon. There sat a cockroach looking right back at him. With somewhat more discretion than was needed, I thought, Willy motioned for Eddie to come over.

Eddie walked over holding a spatula and said, "What's the matter?" Willy looked at him and, not to disturb the other patrons, says quietly "I asked for bacon and eggs. You sold me fucking bacon with legs." He turned over the bacon, exposing the roach. Eddie took his spatula, flicked the roach onto the floor, stepped on it, and walked away. Willy is looking at me and says "What the fuck just happened? Does he expect me to eat this shit?" I reached for napkins to wipe up the coffee I had spit out. I pulled a napkin out of the holder and two more small roaches fall out of it onto the counter. I turned to Willy and said, "I think we're in hell!" He started laughing and said "Let's get the fuck outta here." We threw some money to the waitress and left.

In retrospect, after sharing our morning meal with the six-legged denizens of Eddie's Diner, I would have been much better off heading home and calling off sick. But being raised by parents who instilled in me a strong work ethic, doing that was hardly an option. After arriving at work and checking the job assignment board, I was relieved to see I was scheduled to go out on the building inspector crew. It started to look like the day was turning out to be a good one.

Our job that day was to inspect a line of six ninety-foot tall electrical transmission towers carrying thousands of volts of electricity to supply the cranes at the auxiliary shipping yard. This was a routine inspection, done yearly. Our crew that day consisted of myself, a rigger named John Kloo, and an electrician safety man. My responsibility was to climb and inspect the structural integrity of the towers. I would send any reports of abnormalities or cracked welds via radio to John on the ground, who would then transcribe them into a notebook.

The towers were eighty to ninety feet tall, 4' x 4' wide, cross-hatched by horizontal 3" x 3" angles and diagonal angles welded to the four heavy 6" x 6" angle legs. These towers were usually inspected in the warmer months, but today was a bitterly cold day with the temperature hovering around fifteen degrees. Climbing towers in winter meant heavier clothing, long underwear, and heavy gloves. Climbing and circling the tower to inspect it took much longer.

Before inspection could begin, the electrician would call the substation to shut down the towers that we were inspecting. This was routine and had been done many times before without problems. On this particular morning, due to the frigid weather, John and the electrician took refuge in a heated shanty used by the shipping crews. Clad in heavy lugged sole work boots, jeans, a heavy hooded sweatshirt covered by a military field jacket, and heavy welder's gloves, I began to climb. I left my hard hat with John. It was useless to wear it on the tower. Anything landing on your head from above would probably have been ejected from one of the five million pigeons inhabiting the steel mill during the winter months. If you fell head first from the tower with your hard hat on, it would just become a permanent part of your skull.

I started slowly, circling the tower, visually inspecting the welds. I kept my radio in my jacket chest pocket. The only other tool I carried was a painter's chipping hammer to clear rust away. I had been on the tower for about ninety minutes and had inspected to a height of about fifty feet when I get a call on the radio. "It's break time. Come down and warm up," said John. As I stepped off of the tower, I heard the familiar horn toot of the ARA truck. The company allowed the ARA Company to run a fleet of chuck wagon vehicles throughout the plant to provide coffee and snacks to the employees.   Although there were numerous small "stores" throughout the plant run by entrepreneurial employees, it was usually easier to access the ARA food truck. After a few years of working in the plant their routes and stops were engrained into one's memory.

In the early nineties, a machinist operating a small company store in #2 machine shop sold everything from coffee and cigarettes to aspirin and shoelaces. In the twenty or so years his store was in operation it was reported that he actually made more money running his minimart than he did as a machinist, and machinists at Bethlehem Steel were some of the highest paid employees.

As I finished my hot chocolate and crushed out my Marlboro, it was time to head back up the tower. As I started climbing, revived by caffeine and nicotine, I noticed John and the electrician retiring to their warm shanty. It didn't bother me very much that I was freezing and doing the bulk of the work. As long as the rigger department was in existence, it was always the young riggers who did the climbing, and the old riggers who stayed earthbound. This practice was more than a matter of seniority. It was a show of respect to the older riggers who were our friends and mentors.

I had reached the point I had been at before break time, and resumed the slow and methodical inspection. Circling the tower, I had climbed to about seventy feet when something peculiar began to happen. My radio reception became sketchy at best and static-filled, and the hair on the back of my neck began to literally stand up. About three seconds after reporting this odd phenomenon, a voice came over the radio screaming "Get off the fucking tower! Get off the fucking tower!"

Without reaching for my radio to inquire why, I began the slow climb down. With about twenty feet to the ground, I looked over my shoulder to see our electrician safety man pacing nervously back and forth. When I got to the bottom, I stepped off and slowly walked over to the electrician. "What the fuck happened?" I asked. As if assuming he was going to be punched, he stepped back slightly and said "You were climbing a hot tower."

He was probably a bit confused by the slight smile that appeared on my face. The smile came purely from my thoughts about my guardian angel. He had just saved me about three weeks earlier from igniting myself, and now I was musing whether guardian angels can apply for overtime wages.

My demeanor did change slightly when they explained to me that high voltages, like those running through the wires on my tower, can arc outward ten feet to someone working close to them. Fortunately I had been about twenty feet away when the electrician realized, from my radio call, the danger that I was in. He was relieved when I thanked him for saving my life but became a bit unnerved when I told him to never tell me who had shut down the wrong fucking tower grid at the substation. I would have felt compelled to employ my spud wrench in a way it was never intended for. My guardian angel would get a well-deserved three year respite until he had to go back into action, keeping me alive.

20 GYPSIES AND THIEVES

Early in my career as a rigger I remember walking through #2 Machine shop with several other riggers, on our way to the sintering plant where we were scheduled to work that day. We were very easy to detect from the clanking noise our tools made, swinging from our tool belts. Most riggers strapped on a belt every day containing a varied complement of tools: an eight foot braided nylon safety rope clipped to one of two heavy metal D rings; a leather holster containing a spud wrench for 7/8 bolts and one for ¾ inch bolts; a canvas bolt bag attached to the rear of the tool belt which held a sixteen ounce maul (heavy hammer); a heavy metal chisel; a holster with a bull pin (a heavy twelve inch long tapered pin used for aligning the bolt holes on girders and columns); and a slim eighteen inch pry bar.

Needless to say we weren't stealthy when we moved around. On this particular day, while walking through the #2 shop I heard a machinist shout, "Here come the riggers, hang on to your wallets!" I turned to the rigger next to me and said, "Hey Snapper, what the fuck did he mean by that?" Snapper looked at me and said "It's the rep we have. We're the fuckin thieves and gypsies of the plant." I would soon come to embrace that reputation.

Two or three years prior to working for Bethlehem Steel, I had been thinking about starting a career as a locksmith. I had become intrigued by people who could open locks without keys. I enrolled in a correspondence course and received my first lesson. In reality, I only had taken the course to acquire a student locksmith identity number. At that time lock picks could only be purchased from reputable companies who would only sell to bonded locksmiths or students with a valid ID number. Three weeks later, after my check cleared and my student identification number was verified, I received my first set of lock picks from the Zipf Lock Company of Chicago. One week after this, I dropped my locksmith course, citing financial hardship.

I then began to practice. Padlocks, doorknobs, deadbolts, anything that required a key: I would try to open it. Within a few months, I was quite proficient at surreptitious entry into anything lockable. If you have this ability, one should also possess a strong moral rectitude, for you are walking a narrow line between morality and corruption. I will admit in the many years I have been able to manipulate locks, I probably sit on the 80/20 line, eighty percent being the good side.

While early into my lock picking career, I was dating a young lady who lived in an apartment building. I must have been bragging too much about my new talent, because she asked me how long it would take to get into her apartment, which had a doorknob lock, a deadbolt, and a chain lock. I told her I could break in in under three minutes with a rake pick, a tension wrench, a thumbtack and a rubber band. The bet was on: loser would pay for dinner.

"I only have one rule for this test," she said.

"Ok," I said, "what's the rule?"

"You must try to get into my apartment naked," she said, smiling.

"Are you out of your fucking mind? There are three other apartments in this hall. Besides, it's winter, I'll freeze my balls off."

"Well, I suppose you're not that good!" she said.

That challenge and my gross stupidity overcame my capacity for rational behavior. Three minutes later I was standing there, naked and shivering, two feet from her in a warm apartment with a locked door between us.

Any locksmith will tell you it takes a lot of concentration to pick a lock....with your clothes on. Unless you are a locksmith in a nudist colony, you can't imagine what I went through for the next seven minutes. The doorknob popped in about twenty seconds. The deadbolt was stiffer and took about six minutes to pop. Opening the door four inches, the security chain lock held. Reaching around the door opening, I put the thumbtack about twelve inches past the rail that the lock slid on, then attached the rubber band to it. Simply closing the door, the tension of the rubber band pulled the lock off the slide. I was in. After a warm hug and a trip to Arby's, I was vindicated. We broke up three weeks later. I suppose she didn't want to date someone who was so gullible. A great deal of practice and preposterous feats such as the previous one honed my skills to a fine point.

In the first few months as a rigger, very few of my fellow employees knew of my talents as a lock manipulator. I rarely pulled any jobs off and I never kept a set of lock picks with me. At that time I was merely known as a "scrounger". If any of my friends needed a tool or any other item that was safely locked up, it would miraculously appear within a few days. I always thought of myself as a quasi-Robin Hood, taking from the rich (company) and giving to my union brothers.

I found out rather quickly that an entire underground of misappropriated items existed within the plant. It was as if you combined a Home Depot with the Black Market, but unlike these entities, any item was free. It would not be stretching the truth by any means to say that if everything that was stolen, pilfered, ripped off, boosted or taken without permission from the Bethlehem Steel Plant or corporate offices over the last seventy years were to detach itself from its current location and fly through the heavens returning to Bethlehem Steel, the sunshine would be blocked for months. You would look up and see everything from entire houses to paper clips, airborne. This is the world I dropped into in the summer of 1975.

The shuttle bus which ran throughout the plant became the link to the black market. Its route took it to almost every shop within the plant. If you needed anything, you merely told the driver and within a few days you would have whatever you asked for. In a time before cell phones or the Internet, it was a remarkably efficient system and the only requirement was that if you received anything you were put on a list as a procurer. You may be asked to provide an item or perform a service. Even some of the plant guards were in the system. They were always asking for items but in return they were usually asked to look the other way at certain times.

Out of all the thieves in the system, the riggers were undoubtedly the best. I knew one or two carpenters and pipefitters that achieved high rankings too, but in reality no one could eclipse the riggers and we were damn proud of it. When the secret of my lock picking talents got out, I was besieged with requests. I would usually comply, unless the person asking was a total asshole.

One day I was approached by a rigger foreman who handed me a phone message. It was from Dell, a temporary foreman at the Power House. For the previous two or three years when their senior foreman went on vacation, they would "hire" me to open some of his tool lockers. He was a man who controlled access to anything valuable but wasn't averse to ordering tools and equipment for his own use at home. I contacted Dell and told him that since my "tools" were at home, I couldn't help him until the following day.

The "job" was set for the next day at four when my shift was over. When I arrived the rank and file of the department were lined up like a pack of ravenous hyenas, waiting for lockfest to begin. After opening a few cabinets, mesmerizing everyone watching locks being opened so easily, believing it akin to magic or witchcraft, I had a novel idea.

"Hey, Dell. Where is your boss' personal locker?" I asked.

"In the back office."

I walked to the locker, popped it in about thirty seconds, and looked inside to find a large ring of keys which I unhooked and tossed to Dell. He caught them, smiling, knowing I had just simplified the process.

"Thanks, Neffy, what would you like as payment for your service?" he said, laughing.

"No fee for my union brothers," I said.

"Thanks. Isn't there anything here you could use?"

"Okay," I said. "How about a few drill bits?"

"No problem," he says as he slides open a filing cabinet drawer. He motions to the open drawer and says, "Take what you want: everything from 1/16" to ½"!" The bits were ten to a pack, in small paper envelopes. As I started opening the pack to take out one bit, he reached past and took out eighteen full envelopes, put them in a bag and handed them to me, grinning.

"What the fuck am I going to do with 180 drill bits," I asked.

"Split them up into sets and give them to your rigger buddies," he said.

Opening locks wasn't always for gain. Most of the time I used my talents for helping others: forgotten keys, lost keys, broken keys in locks, or lock outs. A few times they were used entirely for practical jokes.

In 1978 the Rigger Department began losing a substantial part of its workforce due to retirements. A posting was put up to hire twenty-eight riggers. For many years the incentive program (money earned that was added to one's hourly rate) was never equitable for the carpenters. Working on a job with a rigger gang, incentive money for the rigger might add up to three dollars per hour, but the carpenter would receive eighty cents per hour. This caused a mass migration of carpenters into the rigger department. Many of the riggers, including myself, spent time training our carpenter pals in the finer arts of rigger training so they would have an edge on passing the test.

What it also caused was a rift between the division foreman of the riggers, Jim Chlebove, and the carpenter division foreman Phil Prosperi. It's not that they truly liked each other in the first place, but for the rigger boss to "steal" the top nail bangers from the carpenter department just added to the dissension.

Being scheduled to work middle shift (4 PM to 12 AM) one day, I left the welfare room, where I had just changed into my work clothes and headed over to the Saucon rigger building. This building houses the rigger tool room and the carpenters' workshop plus a long row of enclosures along the west wall which contained the clerical offices of the carpenters, riggers, rate setters and pipe shop. Adjacent to the carpenter office was a large walk-in metal cabinet belonging to carpenter boss Prosperi.

As I walked into the building, I stopped to get a pack of smokes from the cigarette machine. "Son of a bitch," I thought. "These pricks just raised the price of smokes from 45 cents to fifty cents a pack." Only a nickel, I thought, but when is this shit going to stop. As I was mentally cursing the bloodsucking cigarette vendor, someone tapped me on the shoulder. It was Richie Check, long-time

Rigger A man, just promoted to temporary rigger foreman. Checky was a great rigger and the kind of a guy you would do anything for.

Checky puts his arm on my shoulder and walks me over to a large wall locker. He points at a large padlock and says, "Can you open that?" I grabbed the lock, and turned it up to look at the keyway. "Three minutes tops," I said and asked "What do you want that's inside?" He grins, and says "I don't want to take anything out…..I want to put something in!"

This was a first for me. "What's the job?" I asked. Pointing down the aisle, he says "See that new fifty gallon water heater sitting there?"

"Yeah, what about it?"

"Well, yesterday there were two, but one was stolen last night!"

"Just the right size water heater for a hunting cabin," I said. "What's the problem, then? Things get boosted all the time around here."

"The plant patrol was here and started an investigation. Prosperi came out and started yelling 'The fucking riggers probably stole it. They steal everything around here!'

"Well, you can't fault the guy for being honest," I said.

"One of our guys on nightshift did steal it. But who the fuck is he to start yelling and blaming us?" Checky said.

"Yeah, you're right, Checky. Who is he to besmirch our stellar reputation? What do you want me to do?" I asked.

"Tonight open Prosperi's locker, put the water heater inside, and lock it up. We'll see what happens tomorrow," he said, laughing.

Inasmuch as I was working middle shift and the investigation of the latest "theft" would not begin until the next morning, I would have to rely on Checky to give me the details on how our prank turned out.

The next day I was sitting on a bench in the welfare room, having a smoke, when I saw Checky come into the room and look around. He saw me sitting there and came over to me smiling ear to ear.

"I suppose your little plan worked out," I said.

"Did it ever!"

"Did they open his locker?" I asked.

"The shit hit the fan about 9 AM. The pipe shop boss reported the theft and two plant patrol cops and Captain Shimko showed up," he said. "Everyone was out of the offices and there were four gangs of riggers there, who just came in for their coffee break. The Captain checked with all of the officers working on the gates last night and every outgoing vehicle was checked. No water heaters left the plant so they assumed it must still be here in one of the lockers. Prosperi's was one of the first ones they opened! When they came to it, Phil said 'That's my locker...it's not in there!' The Captain made him open it anyway. You should have seen his face when he swung open the door. He started yelling that he didn't know how it got in there. The Captain laughed and said 'Don't worry Phil, we're not going to arrest you....Remember yesterday morning when you were screaming about how the riggers were thieves and steal everything?"

'Uh....yeah,' Phil said, turning to see about twenty riggers smiling at him.

"I've been here thirty years and I've learned one thing, Phil. Don't fuck with the riggers, they're vindictive as hell," the Captain said. "You're a lucky man, Phil," he added.

"What do you mean by that?"

"I mean you're lucky they didn't bend you over and shove that water heater up your ass," the Captain said, evoking laughter from the assembled riggers.

"I think it'll be a long time before Phil calls us thieves again," said Checky. He was right, and a few months later the plant patrol Captain received an anonymous bottle of Scotch for Christmas.

21 EXPLOSIONS

Over the course of my life I've seen, been the victim of, and caused a lot of explosions. Things, however, don't always go up after an explosion. I have seen things blow up, things blow down, and things blow sideways. Or all three at once.

I know I am not alone when I say that as a young lad I was fascinated by watching things explode. Early in my childhood that was confined to watching my brothers Tom and Dan setting off firecrackers in July. Being eight and nine years older than me, they were the explosives experts and I was always the spectator. A few years later, in my early teens, I acquired a chemistry set. It is only by the grace of God and the lack of an internet, where explosive formulas can be easily downloaded, that I am still here to write these stories.

Fortunately, having no formulas to work with, most of my concoctions were total duds. My attempt at making gunpowder using the well-known combination of charcoal, saltpeter and sulphur usually fizzled into a rather large, aptly named, stink bomb. Occasionally I would find someone who would sell me a pack of firecrackers or a cherry bomb at an exorbitant price.

Many years later when I became a rigger, June became the magic month to obtain fireworks of any type. You merely had to walk to the shipping yard in the Saucon Division on your lunch break. You would look for a trucker who had come to pick up a load of structural steel.

Checking license plates made the quest much easier. Find any truck with a Southern plate and it was almost certain to have a sleeper compartment full of explosive ordnance at very low prices. Cherry bombs, M80s, quarter sticks, half sticks (rated with the explosive power of half a stick of TNT).

One year I purchased fifty dollars worth of goodies from an Alabama trucker. I had enough explosive power in that shopping bag, had everything gone off simultaneously I would have been launched into a geo-synchronous orbit. This good-ole-boy also threw in a free aerial bomb after I complimented his choice of music when I heard a Willie Nelson tape playing in his cab.

I had always treated anything explosive with the utmost care and respect. It was after I joined the Rigger Department that things would go slightly awry.

My first explosive faux pas came shortly after an older rigger named Luther Weiss (LKW to his friends), explained to me how to concoct a milk carton bomb. All that was required to construct this device was a waxed cardboard one quart milk carton, an oxy/acetylene cutting torch, and some fool to set it off. I obtained the first two items but ego wouldn't let me admit I could possibly be the third. One cool night in October I tested my ego theory. I obtained the milk carton, folded over the top to flatten it out, bored a small quarter-inch hole in the side, pumped some acetylene gas into it and then gave it a shot of oxygen. I then stuffed a small piece of paper towel into the hole to act as a fuse. I lit the fuse and stepped back. "Poof!" Shit, wrong gas mixture. Not being one to be put off by a failure, I spent the next three hours blowing up every milk carton within two square miles, finally finding the correct fuel mixture.

By this time, the crew I was supposed to be working with came back for lunch. I coaxed Dave Brewer, the welder in our crew, to come out and view my latest creation. While he was standing behind me, I lit my cutting torch and proceeded to light my bomb. I stepped back. "The fuse burned out" said Dave. "Relight it." As I clicked my spark lighter to light my cutting torch, I experienced a bit of uneasiness. "Seems like a very short fuse", I thought. "Ahhh, what the hell. I'll just light it and jump back."

I never actually jumped. I never heard the explosion. I only felt the five pound thirty inch long brass torch hitting me in the face and knocking me backwards. Fortunately I was wearing my safety glasses which lessened the damage. The torch did tear a two-inch split in my lower lip. As I turned to look at Dave, he was laughing. "That was great, can you do it again?" Spitting blood, I managed to respond with a hearty 'Fuck you".

The boss came walking out after hearing the explosion.

"Hey, Butch, I have to go up to the dispensary to get my lip sewn up."

"What the fuck happened....did you make another one of those fuckin milk carton bombs? I had a half of a quart of milk in the office refrigerator for my coffee. Did you blow that up, too?"

"No, boss, Dave punched me," I said.

Laughing, Dave said "He blew himself up."

"What the hell are you going to tell the nurse?" asked Butch.

"Fuck it, I'll tell her the truth. I'm German/Irish. The German half made the bomb and told the Irish half to light it. What the fuck is the sense of being half Irish if you can't do something stupid."

Laughing, Butch said "That's the truth, but think of something else and lie to her. They're used to that."

A small lie, a quart of milk for Butch, and four stitches later, my career making milk carton bombs was over.

22 DUTCH

When police officers, firefighters or military combatants wake up every morning, they are aware of the possibility of death or serious injury as a constant in their jobs. The same thing exists in the life of anyone entering a steel mill for work each day. Many mornings, after strapping on my tool belt, checking the job sheet to see who was in my gang, and where I worked that day, I would quietly wonder if I would return home after my shift.

Death can come quickly and from many directions. In the mid-eighties on a bitterly cold January morning, I was heading down Polk Street, heading toward to main gate of the Lehigh plant just off Third St. I was juggling a hot coffee and a cinnamon bun, while trying to dig out my key ring with my brass check (identification) to show the plant patrol guard. As I looked up, I saw Floyd "Dutch" Hahn, standing there, rocking back and forth from one foot to the other trying to keep warm.

"Hey, Floyd? What's up?" I asked.

"I'm running on the ticket for Union elections. Just shakin' a few hands."

"Shit, if you can stand out in fuckin ten degree weather to shake my hand, I can certainly vote for you. Besides, you're a climber, so I'll vote for you twice."

"Dutch" was a wireman. Wiremen were the high-climbing electricians in the plant. There was great mutual admiration between riggers and our "hot wire" brothers. They, like us, performed their jobs at dizzying heights.

"Dutch" laughed, I shook his hand, and then I headed off to the Rigger building to get ready for work. I went out on the job that day as a building inspector with Derwood Johnson. Our job was checking on the structural integrity of the heavy vertical columns under the "Hoover-Mason" trestle on which ore cars ran, from the sintering plant to the blast furnaces, to offload their cargoes of ore pellets.

About 9:30, I climbed down off of the trestle and walked over to the ARA food truck to get a coffee. A few people were milling around and one of the carpenters who was standing there came over and asked me if I knew Floyd Hahn.

"Yeah, I just talked to him three hours ago at the Main Gate."

He looked at me and said, "He's dead!"

My legs got weak. "What happened?"

"Well, nobody knows for sure, but he was on a tower on top of the central tool building, about ninety feet up, and he fell. They took him to St. Luke's, but the guys working with him said he didn't have much chance. They are really taking it hard."

As I walked back to the job I was wondering why God would take such a nice, quiet, soft-spoken guy like "Dutch". After something like this happened, it would really shake you up. Bethlehem Steel never had any program set up to counsel friends and coworkers of someone who lost their life.

There was an incident a few years later where a rigger gang helped to rescue an employee who had third degree burns on ninety per cent of his body and was still alive. I knew these guys and they were some of the toughest bastards in the rigger department. What they saw and heard had really shaken them. They were advised to head up to the plant dispensary to get checked out. When they got there, the doctor was standing there, filling small bottles from a big bottle of valium. Without showing any concern about what happened, he walked over to the men in line and merely handed them each a bottle of valium and said "Take them if you need them and come back to work tomorrow." If he was trying to get a reaction, he succeeded. As he turned and walked away, one of the riggers said "Hey, Doctor Frankenstein! Stick these fuckin M&Ms up your fat ass!" and threw the bottle at him. Everybody walked out the door. There were no repercussions. The incident was written off to the unofficial motto the riggers had adopted from a combat unit in the Vietnam war: "Ne conjuge nobiscum", a loosely translated Latin phrase meaning "Don't fuck with us."

My second "close encounter of the lethal kind" came only about a month after losing our friend Dutch.

I was working in a four-man gang: Mike Leseberg, Bobby Diehl, Willy D. Chain and I. We were working in a "skip tub" at the bottom of the skip, on the B Blast furnace. The skip tub was the vehicle which took the ore up to the top of the furnace. It was basically an open front tub on rails which was about the size of a minivan. After several loading runs, the inside of the tub would begin to wear down. Our job that day was to fit wearing plates inside the tub and weld them into place. At the same time, one hundred and fifty feet above us, two gangs of riggers were working, changing worn-out rails which the skip tub would ride on.

The vertical incline on which the skip tub rode was set at about seventy degrees. I had worked many times on rail changing on the skip, and it really appeared like you were working on a vertical wall. Every movement you made was a calculated and deliberate act. It was a tough enough job on a mild day, but today the high crews were doing it on a day with a wind chill factor of five below. I shuddered, thinking about those guys above us, even though it was about twenty degrees in the pit where we were.

For safety reasons, the previous day the carpenters had built a plank roof over our heads, using heavy timbers and boards. It was sheathed with two levels of two inch spruce planks. These were actually 2" by 12" by 10' long, not the dried-out piss pine you buy at a home improvement store. So with a four inch thick roof over us, we felt safe. We had installed two wearing plates in the tub and now it was Willy's turn to weld them in. Bobby was in the tub with Willy, and Mike and I were standing on a platform above them, with our heads about four inches below our "safety roof".

Mike looked at his watch and said, "It's 9:30, the coffee truck should be out there."

Because it was a repair shift and time was a crucial element, we chose to take our break "on the job". I took orders and headed off to the coffee truck. As I emerged into the sunlight I looked up and saw the gangs working above me. I remember thinking, "those guys must be freezing their nuts off up there."

After picking up four coffees, two cinnamon buns and a pack of Marlboros, I headed back to the pit. I passed the coffee down to Bobby and Willy and climbed back up. I handed Mike his coffee and backed up a few feet to get mine, which I had left sitting on a railing. As I turned, I opened my coffee, took a sip, and heard a loud "THUNNNG". Willy threw his welding hood up and said "What the fuck was that?"

I was standing there with my mouth open, stunned to see twelve inches of a twenty-pound pry bar sticking through the planks over my head, just eighteen inches in front of my face. I looked at Mike and he started laughing.

"Fuck you, asshole, I almost got a frontal lobotomy!"

Willy yells "Christ, Neffy, you got one helluva angel watchin over you!"

I started laughing, picked up a cutting torch and cut off the bar. I kept that piece of steel in my locker for the rest of my career. Nobody ever admitted to losing that pry bar, nor did I ever ask who had. It was not our way. As I sat in Joe's Bar after work, drinking a beer which I rarely did, I wondered. How many cat lives did I have left?

23 WHERE'S MY TORCH

We didn't always have to learn the safe and most efficient ways to perform our various jobs the hard way. Many of the assignments we were sent out on every day as riggers were repetitive, done many times over the years that the plant was active. Safe ways and effective ways had been learned and taught to fellow employees. It was only when the safe procedures were deviated from that things could go terribly wrong. Almost every employee working in a large, dangerous industry learns rather quickly the old axiom of Murphy's Law: if something can go wrong, it usually will go wrong.

Electricity, for example, was not something to be messed with lightly. Most overhead cranes in the Bethlehem plants operated by drawing power from two 3" x 3" feeder rails, mounted parallel along the crane run. Touching or coming in contact with both rails was generally lethal, or if you didn't die you certainly would become top contender for the crown of village idiot.

Termination by electricity was tested on a somewhat smaller scale by the electricians in the sintering plant at the loop substation. It seems that the oversized vermin in the area had chewed through the brick and plastered wall of their lunch room, endeavoring to pick up a quick meal. An overzealous employee decided to rig up a quick rat trap by wiring two metal plates, set two inches apart, to a 440 line. This quick fryer was set adjacent to the rat entry and dosed with peanut butter. Friday, lights out and everybody heads home for the weekend, wondering if their trap would end their pest problem.

It worked. From the length of time it took to hose down the lunch room it was estimated that a rat of rather copious dimensions, similar to a full-grown Chihuahua, had stepped from one plate to the other and into Bethlehem Steel folklore. He was promptly turned into a rather nauseating, multi-colored wallpaper. Realizing their mistake, there was some talk of wiring a transformer to step down the voltage but more discriminating heads prevailed and it was decided just to seal up the hole in the wall.

The feeder rails at the BOF left no room for doubt. Touch any two of these and you would be vaporized. One day we were working on a repair shift at the BOF (Basic Oxygen Furnace) Department. Our job that day was to repair a broken crane rail. The enormous cranes at the BOF had lifting capacities of well over five hundred tons and ran on rails bolted to girders, mounted atop columns sixty feet in the air. The rails were exactly like the rails large electro-diesel trains ride on. The massive electric motors that powered the drive wheels and the lifting hoists drew their electricity from a series of six feeder rails mounted on brackets along the side of the support girders. When active, the feeders supplied thousands of volts to the crane's various systems.

The power used to operate the crane that ran on the rail that we were repairing that day drew such a large amount of electricity that to shut it down completely required four separate safety lock-out points instead of the normal one or two that smaller cranes needed. Locking out a crane simply meant that the foreman on the job would locate the power control box for the crane, pull the switch handle to the "off" position, and put a padlock on it. As per safety regulations, whoever locked out an electrical control box was the only person who could unlock it. To work safely on our job that day, three separate control boxes had to be locked out and a telephone call had to be made to an electrical substation within the plant instructing the operations supervisor to shut down power to our specific location.

Assuming that our rigger foreman "Charly" had shut down the power to the crane feeder rails which were a mere eight feet below our work area, our rigger gang began prepping our job. The crew consisted of our gang leader or "A" man, Dennis Hoffman. I was the burner, or "B" man. Our welder for the day was the talented and fun-loving Pete Beck. All rigger gangs worked for their hourly rate plus incentive, which we simply called "bonus". Since the bosses all knew which jobs would pay the highest bonus, these jobs were given to their favorite "A" riggers. If you worked with one of these favored "A" men, your pay check would show it, with a possible two or three dollars per hour increase.

On a re-railing job a few months before, a foreman had asked Dennis how many rails his gang had replaced during their shift. Dennis replied "Four". In reality, we had only replaced two. It was July, we were seventy feet up on a crane run above fully operating annealing furnaces, and due to these miserably hot and stifling conditions a fierce water hose battle had broken out between the two competing rigger gangs which lasted through most of our eight hour shift. The foreman confronted Dennis in the washroom at the end of the shift about his original answer of four rails. Dennis looked coolly back at him and said, "I guess I lied to you." After that episode, if you happened to be assigned to Dennis' gang, you knew you would be financially fucked. You also knew, however, that you would have a great shift and laugh a lot.

At the start of this particular job, Dennis was on the ground training a new man on how to send up the tools we needed by rope. In every rigger gang the "A" man carried a hand line which was a fifty to seventy five foot manila fiber rope. It had a variety of uses but pulling up tools and equipment to a job site was the main one. On this particular job, we had carried up our personal tools plus an eight inch grinder we would use to smooth out the welds on the rail after Pete was finished welding it. We had already pulled up the welding lead. This was a heavy braided copper wire encased in rubber, about one inch thick, which led from the welding machine on the ground up to the job site. Attached to a high capacity airline was a seventy foot 1 1/2" wide rubber hose, which brought ninety PSI air to power the grinder. After we had finished securing the air hose and welding lead to the building column behind us with small pieces of rope, I coiled up the hand line and, holding one end, I threw it down to the ground man and motioned him to tie my burning torch on and send it up.

The last twenty minutes we had spent pulling up our gear we had believed that the high power feed rails just below us were de-energized. We were sadly mistaken. For some unknown reason our foreman had decided we could work safely while the feed rails were hot. My burning torch was tied on and I started pulling it up slowly. It was constructed of brass, copper and steel, about 22" long and attached to a double set of half inch rubber hoses about eighty feet long. The hoses were connected to adjustable pressure gauges on two separate tanks. One was an oxygen tank and the other was a propane gas tank. As I pulled the torch up close to our level, it was banging up against the bottom feed rail.

About this point in time, our foreman climbs up the ladder and walks over to us. "I just wanted to tell you guys, the crane feed rails are hot. Be careful."

"Great time to tell us," Pete said.

I looked at him and said, "We got most of our gear up, I'm just pulling up my torch now." Now, I'm aware the feed rails have thousands of volts passing through them. As long as my metal torch doesn't contact two rails, I'm safe. I yell down to the ground man to hold the hose and slowly release it, so I can pull it up at an angle, safely clearing the hot feed rails.

As our foreman walks away, and with Pete standing next to me, I begin pulling up the torch. To my disbelief, the ground man lets go of the hose. The torch swings back, up against the feed bars.

The explosion was deafening: a giant ball of fire and sparks erupting eight feet beneath where we stood. We instinctively backed up and stood there. I see the rope I had been pulling up cart wheeling through the air. It landed at my feet, smoldering like a burning fuse. I lift it up, look at it with a stunned face, and turn to Pete. "Where's my fuckin torch?" I said. He just looked at me and started laughing. I turned around to see the foreman running back toward us, ready to start screaming at us. He became more incensed when he saw us laughing. I thought to myself, "Don't you say a fuckin thing to us. You didn't lock them out!" As if reading my mind, he stopped in his tracks, turned, and walked away.

The thirty or so men who had been working on the floor below, before running for their lives, started filtering back. Someone yelled up, "You fuckin riggers are crazy." I looked at Pete and he said, "Like we never heard that before." Dennis yelled up, "I'm going to get another torch!" I sat down, lit up a smoke, and thought

"What a rush!"

24 GAS SCHOOL

In the late seventies, anyone in the various departments of the Service Division (riggers, pipefitters, carpenters) who were previously "gas trained" had to be retrained in the use of the new SCBA (self-contained breathing apparatus). For many years riggers had the dubious and dangerous job of patching the gas lines which ran all the way from the coke ovens on the border of Hellertown to the blast furnaces in South Bethlehem. These thirty inch pipes, originally installed in the 1930s, were constantly developing holes which spewed gas. This stuff was mostly carbon monoxide, highly flammable, and quite deadly.

Before the advent of the SCBA we used different types of breathing apparatuses. The first one I was trained to use looked like something doughboys would wear in the trenches of World War I to survive gas attacks. It was worn on the chest and consisted of two rubber bladders or "lungs" with a canister of crystals, similar to a brandy flask, which created oxygen. You pierced the seal with your facemask hose, screwed it on the canister, tightened your facemask, and proceeded to fall flat on your face because this contraption made you top heavy. Only workers with enormous backsides as counterweights could use it, and they usually ventured only a few feet before piercing the rubber lungs on something sharp, rendering it useless. It was eventually tossed onto the scrap pile of bad inventions, to the delight of many riggers, who all agreed "it made you look like a jackass" if you wore it.

We did have an alternative, nearly as suspect, "the fresh air mask". This was simply a rubber mask with a plexiglass face shield attached to a one-inch hose running to a large tank of fresh air. The tank was monitored by a worker called a "gas checker" from the combustion department. These gentlemen were very dedicated to their jobs, and we appreciated it very much. In essence, they kept you alive. It was quite usual, though, that during your shift another rigger would deliberately stand on your hose, watching you gasp for air, wriggling like a trout on a line. You never complained, because you were working in the toughest department with the craziest bunch of bastards at Bethlehem Steel. Complaining would show weakness, resulting in harsher horseplay. Much better to suck it up and keep your mouth shut.

One chilly autumn Tuesday morning I was sitting in the washroom, smoking a cigarette and drinking a cup of Freddy the tool room man's coffee. I use the word coffee loosely. It resembled coffee to a certain degree, but tasted more like the dirty old rags he used to wash the pot. But with enough Coffeemate and sugar it was palatable.

Ernie the rigger foreman, came up to me. "Neffy, you're scheduled to go to gas school today."

"Aw, c'mon Ernie, I'm half in the bag. I was watching Monday night football till 1 AM and I only got three hours sleep!"

"I can see that," he replied. "Your eyes look like two piss holes in the snow."

"Alright," I muttered, "Maybe it will wake me up. Who's going with me?"

Ernie gave a wry smile. "Draz and Astronaut John."

Not bad. Two good riggers I liked.

Draz was from Minersville. He was a quiet guy who had a remarkable thermos bottle. It held about two pints, but amazingly it never ran out. The guys dubbed it "the continuous pour" after a similarly called steel-making process. He was a good rigger who drove about seventy miles to work each day. Anyone who would do that to feed his family had my admiration.

Astronaut John was an enigma. His nickname had been given to him after a bizarre incident. One day John was hooking up a cable attached to a beam. The overhead crane man watched John attach the cable to the hook on the crane block, then pushed the lever to raise the load. But he hadn't checked to see if John was clear, and didn't notice that the sleeve of John's welding glove had slipped over the hook. The load went up fifteen feet and proceeded to travel down the shop, with John dangling from it. He hung on for about two hundred feet before the crane operator realized what was happening, and lowered John down. But he had five very angry riggers looking up at him. Prudently, he remained on his crane and wouldn't come down until the end of his shift. Someone mentioned that John had resembled an astronaut on liftoff. The name stuck.

Everyone reading this has probably eaten a bowl of Cheerios. You are almost finished and you have a half bowl of milk and ten Cheerios left. When you try to scoop all ten up, one invariably swims to the other side of the bowl to do its own thing. That Cheerio was John. John was tough. He was a Marine combat veteran of WWII. As with many others from the "greatest generation", fighting for his country on some God forsaken Pacific atoll with death all around him had its effects, and he had come home a much-changed man. If you worked in a gang with John, he sometimes seemed to be in his own little world.

So off we three headed to gas school, happy to be free of our fifteen-pound tool belts for once. To train us properly, the company had converted an old office building behind the unused old #3 open hearth, just west of "A" blast furnace, to a gas school training facility. Gas school was set up in two large rooms. The instructor was in the first room waiting for us. Since this was one of the first classes, the corporation had sent some suit from the offices to see how the training was going. John, Draz and I signed up on the roster and began training.

First we were shown the new SCBA unit. It consisted of a rubber full-shield mask, backpack tank, and on the hip belt a small five-minute escape tank. All the while we were being shown the proper use and procedure for employing this unit, I kept looking over at John. He seemed off in his own little world again. He was only a few years from retirement so he wasn't too concerned if he passed or failed the test. Most probably, he wouldn't have to wear one of these masks for the rest of his time in the plant.

Once we had been trained in strapping on the pack, adjusting the mask, turning on the air tank, and checking the seals, we were told to take a ten-minute break. Draz had a coffee. I had a smoke. John wandered around. The second part of our training was coming up.

I was confident that I wouldn't screw up, but I asked Draz what he thought. "I'll do OK, but I'm not sure how much John was paying attention." I eyed John drifting randomly around the room. "I hope the fuck he did or we're going to look like the Three Stooges!" I said.

The second part of the test began. The object of the training was to rescue a fully dressed dummy from somewhere in the training room. With gear on, we would enter the room, climb some stairs, turn a wheel to close a valve on a simulated 36" gas pipe, search for the victim, and then carry him out. Not too hard of a task, until we were told that the room would be filled with smoke. Oh, shit. "Oh, and by the way," the instructor said. "During the test one of your tanks is going to run out of air, and that guy is going to have to switch to his escape bottle."

We suit up and check each others' gear. The trainer throws a smoke bomb into the room and waits until it fills up. With about twelve inches of visibility, we enter the room. Draz is in front. I'm in the middle. I look for John, who is supposed to be behind me and he is nowhere to be seen. Draz and I mount the platform, turn the valve off and start looking for the victim. That's when we locate John. Being ever the Good Samaritan, he has gone straight for the victim.

The only problem is, he has gotten to the victim just as his air supply runs out. The bell on his tank starts ringing and he takes his last breath. I look at Draz and say, "Oh, fuck." Draz yells "We've got to get to him!" Before we can, though, John's Marine Corps training kicks in. "Adapt and overcome." Unable to breathe and flopping around, he slips off his tank, rips off the mask, and heads to a window, all the while sucking in smoke and coughing. He lifts his tank and smashes out the window. Sticking his head out and taking a few breaths, he comes back in, grabs the dummy, and throws it out the window. Then he jumps out after it, and starts strolling back to the Rigger building.

Draz and I sit down, laughing so hard we almost piss our pants. We hear the overhead fans go on and two minutes later the smoke clears and the door opens. The trainer and the suit come in. Draz and I struggle to regain our composure. The trainer looks at the window and at us and says "What the hell happened here?" The suit looks at the roster on his clipboard, looks at me, and says "What's your name?" I point at myself and say "Larry." I point at Draz and say "He's Moe. And Curly went out the fuckin' window."

They turned three colors of red, and the suit said "You fucking riggers are crazy." I looked at him and said "Hey, pal, we got sensitive feelings. And we're not crazy. But most of us are dangerously eccentric. By the way, did we pass?" The suit pointed to the door and said "Get the fuck out!"

As we were walking out, I heard them discussing bringing John back for retraining. I turned and said "Excuse me gentlemen, but if you bring John back here, you very well might be the next fuckin dummy he throws out the fuckin window." I suppose they were too afraid to bring John back to school, so we all got a passing mark two days later. The carpenters installed a new window, and when the story got around, Astronaut John became an icon in Bethlehem Steel folklore.

25 THE TOMATO

In August '75, a few months after I had started working in the Rigger Department, we were working a repair shift at the sintering plant. It was a miserably hot and dusty day. I looked over and noticed two laborers covered in ore dust from head to toe. They were fighting a losing battle trying to clean up the yard.

Taking a break, one of the laborers sat down, took off the hard hat, and lit up a smoke.

"Hey, Steve, that's a woman," I said to our "A" man, Steve Gombosi.

"Yeah," he said, "Her name is Brenda."

When she heard her name, she came walking over. Being the only female within five miles, she was immediately surrounded by the eight riggers working in the area.

"What department are you guys in?" she asked.

"We're riggers," someone answered. "We do all of the high work and heavy work!"

One of the older riggers, Frank, said "If you like to climb, why don't you transfer into our department?"

"Are there any openings?"

"We're still looking for another apprentice," I said.

"Maybe I'll give it a shot." As she walked back to her job, Frank and Steve started laughing.

"What's so funny?" I asked.

"George or Jimmy would never let her in…..they're old school." Steve said.

To understand the tough opposition Brenda was going to have, I must first explain who she was up against. Jim Chlebove and George Kotich were our senior foremen, Jim being our Division Foreman and George being our General Foreman. Jim stayed away from most of the day-to-day jobs, so he handed the whip to George to handle the riggers working out of the Lehigh Division. I worked with George for the last seven or eight years of his Bethlehem Steel career. He was alternately loved or hated by his men. I realized rather early on that he was a rather large gruff teddy bear, but vindictive as hell. After Sesame Street made its debut in 1971, someone hung the nickname "Oscar the Grouch" on him, which he accepted proudly. So from then on he was called "Oscar" or "The Big O".

He playfully accepted the tricks we constantly played on him. While working middle shifts (4 PM to 12 AM), access to the office was quite easy and with no one there, we were free to wreak havoc. We would rub carbon paper on The big O's hard hat liner, superglue his coffee spoon to his mug and his mug to his desk, or unscrew the mouthpiece from his rotary phone, remove it, and put it in his desk drawer. It was always just playful fun and George went along with it because he knew that we always gave one hundred per cent on the jobs we did, which made him look good to the brass hats at the top of the ladder. Then the proverbial shit hit the fan. A rigger who had come from the Coke Works Division to work a double shift changed everything.

Ronald "Fensty" Fenstermacher decided that it would be a novel idea to stretch plastic kitchen wrap very tightly over the bowel of the office toilet. Knowing that there were no women working there, and that the bosses were too lazy to lift the seat, it was the perfect ruse. At some time the following morning George went in to evacuate his habitual three cups of morning coffee, and found it promptly trying to return from whence it came.

After pissing all over himself, he went ballistic. The next few months George cracked down. Extended coffee breaks and lunches were curtailed. Starting and quitting times were strictly enforced. Overtime wages diminished. This enraged most of the older riggers who aimed their anger at Fensty. We younger riggers were also pissed off, but for an entirely different reason. We were angry at ourselves for not being the first ones to concoct such a worthy gag.

This was about the time that Brenda decided to join the rigger department. She had a very limited amount of seniority, having only started working a few months before. So we were surprised to find that she was given the last apprenticeship, much to the disdain of supervision but to the delight of the riggers.

On a hot and steamy August morning, I was geared up and heading out the door to go to "E" blast furnace for my shift. "Oscar" stuck his head out of the office door. He motioned to me to come in. It was like I had walked into a foreman's meeting. Sitting in the middle of the group was our Division Foreman, Jim Chlebove. Looking up at me he said, "The consensus here is that you are one of the better climbers in the department."

"If you're looking for a climber, Fritz Werner is the best," I said. "He's twenty years older than me and he can out climb me on my best day. What's the job?"

"We're giving the new rigger, Brenda, a climbing test," George said. "We simply want you to climb with her."

"What's she climbing?"

George, pointing out of the window, says "E Furnace, High Stack."

I looked at George and said, "My climbing test was that twenty foot column across the street at the Powerhouse. You want to have her haul her ass up a 260 foot stack for her test?"

"That's her test," George said.

"You guys are really trying to fuck her over."

"That'll be enough!" said a voice from the group. I looked over at a three piece tailored suit, possibly a VP of Bethlehem Steel's HR Division. Before I could ask him if he had ever climbed anything higher than a bar stool, another foreman cut in.

"Neffy, did you ever climb one of the high stacks?" he asked.

"Once," I replied. "To rig a cable for the painting contractor. It took about twenty-five minutes and two cigarette breaks to get up there."

"Do you want the job?" he asked.

"When?"

"Tomorrow morning, tool belt and safety gear."

"OK."

The next morning dawned somewhat hotter than the previous one. As I rolled over in bed to shut off the alarm, I remembered about agreeing to shepherd Brenda up the stack. I was hoping that she wouldn't freeze or faint. If she fainted there was a chance she would fall and land on me.

The "E" furnace stack which we were to climb in 1975 is still visible today. One unique feature of the straight high stacks (which we referred to as "needles") was that, if you opened the hearth door at its base, crawled in, and lay on your back looking up the stack, you would see a night sky even on a bright day. Evidently the stack was so high, sunlight couldn't penetrate to the hearth.

The stacks had a twenty-five to thirty foot diameter at the base, and about a six foot diameter at the top, with a two-course brick liner. The high stack we were about to climb was approximately 270' tall, and unknown to Brenda the stack swayed, even in a moderate breeze. I had found this little detail out a few months earlier while rigging a seat hoist cable for an outside painting contractor. Sitting atop the stack, I realized that the perch I was riding was gently swaying about twelve to eighteen inches in a rather slight fifteen to twenty mile-an-hour breeze. After a few seconds of vertigo I made the adjustment, tied my safety rope to the top welded rung of the ladder, and finished my task.

On the morning of the big climb, I met Brenda on the walkway that comes off "E" furnace and is attached to the stack. She was standing there smoking a cigarette and leaning on the hand railing, dressed in her full rigger regalia: work belt, bolt bag, holster with a ¾ spud wrench and a twelve inch adjustable wrench, safety rope and a sixteen oz hand hammer. Being only about 5'4" and one hundred pounds, she looked more like a tool belt wearing a woman. It was tough enough for me, at 6'3" and 210 pounds, to haul my ass up that stack wearing all my gear. I truly never thought that she would ever make it.

"Are you ready to climb?" I asked her, while looking at the fifteen pounds of hardware strapped to her.

"Yeah," she said, flicking her cigarette over the safety railing and watching it land on the passing ore car beneath us.

"How do you want to do this?" she asked.

"You are the lead climber and I'm your backup," I said, adding "Take your time."

"You think I'll make it?"

"Why the fuck not! Climb slow and steady.....you'll feel it in your arms, first. If you tire, lean back against the safety barrel and shake out your arms. Besides. They didn't give you a time limit, so don't worry."

She grabbed the first rung of the ladder.

"If you start to cramp up, yell down to me. I have a quart of water in my bolt bag."

"Okay," she said as she started the climb. I waited till she had climbed up to about twenty feet and grabbed the ladder.

"Why the fuck did I volunteer to do this?" I thought as I started climbing. Without any type of warm up, my arms and shoulders started burning at about the one hundred foot level when I heard Brenda yell down to me to ask if we could rest.

"Absolutely," I yelled back, reaching for a Marlboro Light. As I lit up, I heard her say "Oh shit, I dropped my lighter."

"Do you want to climb back down to get it?"

"Are you out of your fuckin mind?" she yelled.

I smiled, thinking "Well, she has the mouth to be a rigger."

"Hold on, I'll climb up to you," I said. As I approached her to light up her cigarette, I looked over my shoulder and said "I don't fuckin believe this."

She looked down and asked "What's wrong?"

"Look behind you," I said.

During our climb up the ladder, we had our backs to the rigger washroom and office building, which was about two hundred yards behind us. There, sitting on lawn chairs, were six or seven foremen and suits from the main office, watching us with binoculars as we climbed the stack.

"We should moon those assholes!" Brenda said, laughing.

"Hey, focus on the climb," I said. "The best way to fuck them is to finish it. That fat fuck in the blue suit from HR would probably shit in his pants if he was up here with us."

We had our laugh and started climbing again. I let her get about thirty feet above me. By now we were both soaked through our clothing and she was starting to drip on me. I didn't mind that so much, but it made me look up to see her spud wrench hanging upside down in its leather holder. The gear they had issued to her was new and the leather was stiff. While she was climbing it had gotten caught on the safety barrel that surrounded us.

"Brenda, your spud wrench is about to fall out of its holster!" I yelled. In the tight confines of the ladder and barrel, she did make an effort to retrieve it, but it fell. With nowhere to go I tried to suck my entire body into my hard hat, like a frightened turtle. But by the grace of God the wrench hit a ladder rung about two feet over my head and careened out into the stratosphere.

I looked up and she's looking at me with an "oops" half-grin on her face.

"Where did my wrench go?" she asked in a sheepish voice.

Gathering all of the calmness I could muster, I looked up at her. "I suppose if your wrench isn't sticking in my fucking head, then it probably fell to earth somewhere."

"Are you pissed off?"

"No, but you owe my guardian angel a case of beer."

It took another fifteen minutes to reach the top. Brenda was sitting on the stack ring and I was sitting on the top edge of the safety barrel. We tied off with our safety ropes and lit up cigarettes. We allowed ourselves a wave to the binocular gang and sat there admiring the beautiful view.

"Congratulations," I said, looking over at Brenda.

"What for?"

"Out of the 170 riggers working here, you are in a select group of about ten that ever climbed up here," I said.

So with a combination of pride and fatigue we started back down. After explaining to Brenda that I thought I had slightly more control of my tools, I let her climb down first. When we got down to the bridge level we were greeted by George and Jim, our foremen. George was chewing on his ever-present cigar.

"It took you over forty minutes to get up there," George said.

"I didn't know there was a time limit on us," I said.

They both glared at us, did an about-face, and walked away grumbling.

"Why were they pissed off?" Brenda asked.

"You beat them at their own game. Welcome aboard, rigger," I said.

Two weeks later, working middle shift, I broke into the foreman's office, picked the padlock on the tool locker, and boosted a new spud wrench for Brenda. She was still using it when the plant shut down twenty-five years later.

26 ATTITUDE ADJUSTMENT

I have always avoided violence and advocated humor to rectify misunderstandings. This worked fairly well throughout my early years, and still worked most of the time at work. The Rigger Department, however, had its own basic code of ethics. Simply put, if you did something stupid…..you got your ass kicked. I was never one to be spoiling for a fight, but I learned early on that if someone pushed I needed to immediately push right back or risk getting run right over.

This way of dealing with the world became engrained and instinctual for me, both inside and outside the plant. When I married, that zone of protection widened to enclose my wife, and when my sons were born it widened yet further to become an umbrella of safety wrapped around them. Anyone violating that space was going to get their ass kicked.

My sons, of course, were a special and precious responsibility. But watching my wife in labor and delivering them had also made me realize that women are not equal to men. They are vastly superior. I came to the conclusion that if it was up to men to create new life and give birth, there would only be about twelve people living in North America. My respect for not only my wife but for all women rose exponentially.

I had been working in the Rigger Department for about ten years when this set of hard-wired instincts played out in my life. I had taken my sons, aged five and eleven months to a restaurant for dinner. Jared, my oldest son, and I sat in a booth. Adam sat in a child's chair. While we were happily enjoying our meal, two men and a woman, probably university students, sat down at an adjacent booth. They were obviously drunk or stoned, or both. I really didn't care too much that when their food arrived they started a food fight. The restaurant manager noticed their behavior and shrugged it off.

What these young people didn't notice was that they were getting a bit too close to the protective sphere around my children. I took the soft approach, and politely asked them to stop throwing food. The young man facing me, evidently bolstered by a few beers, looked up at me and said "Fuck you, asshole." Having heard that familiar phrase from co-workers on a daily basis, and having used it frequently myself at work, I was hardly impressed.

But then he did the unthinkable. He took a pickle from his burger and threw it at me. It struck Adam. I closed the ten feet between us, I believe, before the pickle hit the floor. Conveniently, he had long hair, which I grabbed and used to slam his head onto the table, thus ending the food fight.

He was fortunate. I really don't know if it was ketchup or blood on his face, but the double bun of his Big Mac had saved him from a broken nose. I quietly asked him to apologize to my sons, which he did. Being engrossed in their "Happy Meal" toys, they were oblivious to the apology. The trio left quietly with a lesson learned. The manager came over and thanked me, and my sons scored a free extra toy.

I did feel some remorse for my actions, but wrote the incident off to paternal protective instinct. From my point of view, that young man was fortunate to have incurred my rage. If their mother had been with the boys, the young man would have left the restaurant in a body bag.

Earlier in my rigger career I had witnessed a violent act which demonstrated that I was not the only one in the department with a deep-seated respect for women, a distaste for bullies, and an instinct for rough justice. In the late seventies most of the riggers in the plant were working in the Lehigh Division on a blast furnace rebuild. Other departments, however, were laying off employees. Some of these workers opted to take temporary jobs and joined our department. They were used as ground men only, which delighted them. Few wanted to work 250 feet up on the furnaces or stacks. We started the rebuild on a Monday with a new man in our gang. I truly can't remember his name but I do remember his somewhat obnoxious behavior that day. Then, he didn't show up for work on Tuesday or Wednesday. Actually, nobody really missed him.

In the interest of discretion, the individual riggers involved in this incident shall remain nameless. The temporary employee came back to work on Thursday morning. He was a bit late showing up in the washroom to change into his work clothes. I overheard him talking to the tool room man.

"Where the hell were you? Haven't seen you since Monday," said the tool room man.

"I was in jail," said the temp.

"What the fuck for?"

"I got in a fight with my wife."

"I argue all the time with my wife and never went to jail," said the tool room man, with a smile.

"She pissed me off, so I hit her. Broke her jaw," said the temp with a chuckle.

There were still about five riggers in the washroom, most having gone out on their jobs. Everyone still there had overheard what he had said except Rigger One.

"Hey Neffy, what did he say?" asked One.

"He hit his wife and broke her jaw," I said. "What a fuckin asshole."

I was not alone that day in being appalled at what he had done, and it made it worse that he was laughing about it. To me, he was a fucking wife beater that needed a lesson. I can't speak for what the other guys felt. But for whatever reasons, everyone who had overheard this asshole agreed that he ran the needle on the "I need my ass kicked meter" well past ten.

There were a few suggestions. Rigger Two wanted to nail his balls to the bench. Rigger Three wanted to just romp and stomp on him. Simple but effective. It was quiet and unassuming Rigger Four who walked out into the tool room, reached into a bolt barrel, and came out with a one inch by four inch bolt wrapped in his fist. "I'm only gonna adjust his attitude," he said with a wry smile as he walked past us, heading to the back of the washroom where the wife beater was.

He walked over to him, stood in front of him, and said "What did you do?" like a judge asking a defendant to repeat his confession. The wife beater retold his story, still with a grin on his face.

"You are a fuckin cowardly piece of shit!" said Rigger Four.

Then the wife beater responded with a "fuck you!"

We all looked at this guy, not believing what he had just said. Who in their right fuckin mind would say "fuck you" to someone standing in front of him with a loaded fist. He either had brass balls or the I.Q. of a tree stump.

Rigger Four said "What?"

The response was the same: a "fuck…" The "you" was drowned out by the noise of his jaw shattering, eerily like the noise of a jar of pennies being dropped on the floor. As he lay sideways on the bench, Rigger Four grabbed him by the lapels of his work jacket and, almost gently, pulled him up off the bench until they were face to face.

"Now you know how your wife feels, tough guy," whispered Four. Then he laid the kid back down on the bench and walked away.

"Hey, Four, I really don't think he heard you. He's out fuckin cold," I said.

"Knocked out my ass, this fucker is gone. Hey Four I think you fuckin killed him," said Rigger Three.

"So what….fuck him, the wife-beating piece of shit," said Four.

Three reminded me I was an EMT. "Check him out." Walking over to him, I knelt down to give him my best EMT "primary survey". For the past two years I had been an EMT and had gone to many accident scenes, so checking this guy was rather routine. I borrowed a flashlight and checked his pupils and airway.

"How does he look?" asked Rigger Two.

"He's still alive," I said. "But I think that fuckin punch rearranged his DNA."

Rigger Four smiled, either because he was relieved he hadn't killed the kid, or because he was pleased with my description of his punch.

"It would probably be a good idea to call for an ambulance," I suggested.

"Fuck the ambulance," said Rigger Three. "Throw his ass on a pallet and use the forklift!" This got a chuckle from everyone. About this time the rigger general foreman, as always chewing on a cigar, came out of the office.

"What the hell is going on," he asked as he walked toward us. "Why aren't you guys over on the job." Looking down, he answered his own question. "All right, what the fuck happened?" he asked.

Everyone just looked back at him and shrugged. He knew us well enough to know that no one would talk. That was partially because we were union brothers, but more so because we were riggers.

"Hey, TRM," said the boss. "Throw a bucket of water on him and hose the blood down the drain."

"Hey, boss, I think the kid lost a couple of teeth," I said.

Looking from me to the tool room man, he added, "Find his fuckin teeth!"

"Fuck that," said the TRM. "I ain't crawling around on the fuckin floor looking for this assholes' teeth. Besides, they're probably under the lockers and I ain't stickin my hand under there. I saw a rat under there the other day."

"Okay, okay, just clean up the blood," said the boss. Looking at us all, he said "You guys get out on the job. I'll call for the ambulance for this guy." Rigger foremen were adept at covering for the sins of the riggers, and fortunately this guy was the best at it.

We all thanked him and got the hell out of there.

I can only assume that this guy mistakenly thought that because he was working in a department with the reputation for having some of the toughest and craziest guys in the plant, we would condone what he had done to his wife. He was vastly mistaken. I hope that after drinking his meals for six months, he may have realized that what he did was terribly wrong.

After a few months he was released by the plant doctor to return to work with us. He chose instead to take unemployment compensation. He did return to his old job eventually, and we would see him occasionally, but he always seemed to vanish if a rigger crew passed through his department. Most probably he couldn't remember which rigger it was who had become his wife's avenging angel. Perhaps what happened did adjust his attitude.

27 BANISHED TO THE GULAG

In the early eighties the old regime of Rigger foremen became eligible to retire. These were the foremen that I had worked for when I left the 42" Mill and began my career as a rigger. These were men from the greatest generation: ex-paratroopers, navy divers and Marines. They were tough, hard men, in a tough hard business. During your shift you did what they said, not just because they told you to do it, but because you learned quite early that they knew how to survive in a very dangerous industry. We had a high percentage of foremen who had come up through the ranks and you had to be tough to make it as a rigger.

I learned how vindictive our general foreman was on one day in mid-August 1976. We had been working for the previous miserably hot two weeks on a ball-busting job at the Drop Forge Department. Even some of the old timers had not seen a job as tough as this one for many years. Our job was to move a three hundred ton block of steel from a specially built railroad flatcar onto greased skids and into a building. It was an anvil for the Number 3 Drop Forge hammer. The steel block measured 10' x 10' x 8'.

When I first walked onto the job I groaned when I saw that immense block. I turned to our foreman Ernie Smith and said, "How the fuck are we going to move this?"

"Chain blocks and a lot of muscle," he said.

After our welders attached two heavy clips to the anvil, we

hooked up to fifty-ton chain blocks and started dragging the anvil. The chain blocks were basically hoists which were usually used in a vertical application to lift heavy loads. On this job, we were using them horizontally to drag the anvil into place, pulling a looped chain around a sprocket wheel attached to gear wheels which either would raise or lower the load chain.

We worked two four-man rigger gangs round the clock, for five days and had succeeded in moving the anvil twenty feet, with another sixty feet to go. About this time our general Foreman, George, walks over to me and hands me a green note pad.

"Neffy, greenslip all of the extra work the gang does on your shift today," he said.

A greenslip was a list of all of the work that was done on your job that wasn't written down on the job plan. Most jobs we did as riggers had usually been done in previous years by previous rigger gangs, so it usually had been written down. The greenslip was given to the rate setters who adjusted the incentive money you would receive over and above your basic hourly rate. It was the foreman's job to write the greenslips, but George didn't want to hang around on such a hot day. I decided, then, to have a little fun with him, never realizing how vindictive he could be. I knew he would review what I had written, but I assumed he wouldn't look past the second page of the slips, which normally added up to five or six.

On the first two pages I wrote down the actual extra work that we completed. But on the third page I exercised my budding literary side.

"Under the constant battering of the unrelenting sun and the sting of the overseers lash, riggers, toiling like the slaves of Ancient Egypt, beaten but not broken, dragged the enormous block into place."

The repercussions appeared two days later when I was called into the division foreman's office. Apparently, my essay had gone further up the ladder than I thought. While I stood in the division foreman's office, he opened his door and called George in.

"This kid is a helluva writer!" he said, laughing.

George was standing there, glaring at me, nodding his head up and down. The next morning, on the bulletin board in our washroom, was my transfer slip to the Coke Oven Division Rigger

Department. I had been sent to the Gulag. I spent the next eighteen months surviving in that toxic hell hole.

At this point in time, the Coke Oven Division had very little pollution control as any workers or nearby residents would readily attest to. My deepest respect goes out to those workers who chose to work there to give their families a better life, knowing that their own lives would inevitably be cut short.

On one of my first days there, I decided to take a stroll on my lunch break to visit the infamous "Veronica Lake". In the forties someone had decided to name it after the voluptuous movie star. It's probably a good thing she never found out about this dubious accolade, or she would have sued Bethlehem Steel.

The "lake" for use of a better word sat in a natural depression in the earth, located on the northeast edge of the border between the Coke Ovens and the East Lehigh Divisions of the pant. It was about sixty or seventy yards across at its widest point and one of the most vile, disgusting places on earth. It was comprised of natural rainfall and every toxic article that the company wanted to dispose of: car batteries, diesel fuel, asbestos, transformer oil, coolants, sludge, pesticides, and many other nasty things were dumped into it. It was surrounded by stunted weeds and cattails, and had a small dock where trucks would back up to unload.

I walked down the dirt road and was standing on the dock, smoking a cigarette, when I heard a fork lift coming up behind me. I turned to see the driver wearing a one-piece disposable paper suit and a full face shield canister respirator. As he jumped off his fork lift, he pulled off his respirator and came over to me.

"Rigger?" he asked.

"Yeah. Just transferred in from Lehigh Division."

"Do you like our little fishing hole?" he asked, laughing.

"From the smell and the look of this place, I'm thinking nothing would live here."

He looked at me and said, "Boy, if you fell in that fuckin pit, that slimy shit would butt fuck your DNA."

Eloquently put, I thought.

"We get ducks and geese that think it looks like a great place to land, and occasionally do. I keep a 22 caliber rifle in my locker. When they land, they're fucked. They can't get out. They get sucked down. I put them out of their misery," he said.

After chatting for a few more minutes, I walked back to the lunch room and asked Mike Shulz, the foreman, for the best respirator he had and wore that thing for the next eighteen months until I returned to the Lehigh Division.

28 BRAD JONES & THE STEEL CAGE MATCH

The old regime of rigger foremen who were working when I started as a rigger in 1975 had either died or retired by the early 1980's. After they left, we were led by a few younger foremen who mostly started at Bethlehem Steel through the "Loop" program and had been trained as engineers. We saw them on a regular basis on various jobs, but they never really had the potential to lead the Rigger department.

It was paramount to have respect from the crews. Our regular foremen who oversaw that day-to-day jobs were completed had been riggers for many years before being made salaried foremen. They had the respect of their crews, having worked side by side with them for many years.

Jack Walters, an old school Marine, was a particularly well-liked foreman. Jack was as strong as an ox, a human gorilla with a great sense of humor, who led his crews mostly by example. If a job wasn't going too well, Jack was a boss who would take off his green foreman's helmet and be the first one to grab a sledgehammer. In retrospect, most of his gangs did what he asked of them because we were not fond of having our arms or legs torn off.

Harold "Butch" Horn was another foreman who was well respected by his rigger buddies. Butch was tough, but had a natural, easy way about him. On difficult jobs he never lost his cool and he would occasionally go out for beers with us after work. Most of the riggers thought of Butch more as a friend than a boss.

Around 1983, Brad Jones became our new General Foreman. If you could teleport the crazy fucking rigger crews and Brad Jones from the 1980's back to Tortuga in the mid-1600s, they would have fit right in. Brad was our "Captain Jack Sparrow". Our new boss was a hard-drinkin', tobacco-chewin', woman lovin' guy who didn't give a rat's fucking ass about the Bethlehem Steel. At last, we had a captain whom the thieves and pirates of the Rigger Department could sail with!

Upon becoming our general foreman, Brad had shown us he had his own way of doing things. For many years he had known the reputation of the Rigger Department. He had been the General Foreman of the Labor Department of the Service Division prior to coming over to join us. We had worked closely with his labor gang unit on many occasions. Knowing the riggers' reputations as consummate thieves, he was determined to protect anything of value within our department.

In the Lehigh Rigger Department building which housed his office, he began construction of a heavy duty "cage" where all things that he deemed precious would be stored. This building contained offices, our "welfare room" for showers and changing clothes, and a tool room. It's still visible today, adjacent to the Channel 39 studio at Levitt Pavillion. Shortly after completion of this ultra-secure facility, Brad went to Cantelmi's Hardware store and purchased the most enormous padlock I have ever seen, placed it on the massive sliding door, and returned to his office with an overwhelming sense of accomplishment.

This was to be dashed upon the rocks a few hours later. We entered our tool room after completing a repair shift at the blast furnaces about 3:45, to see that our new boss had completed his supermax containment facility. Rigger Bob Schleicher, lighting up a cigarette, turned to me and asked, "Can you open that," pointing to the padlock.

"I'll give it a try," I said, retrieving a rake pick and tension wrench that were taped inside the shell of my hard hat. After manipulating the lock, I was surprised to see the cylinder spin and the lock pop open in slightly under ten seconds, much to the amazement and laughter of the assembled riggers milling about.

"What should I do with it?" I asked.

After a little debate, it was decided that someone should present it to our new boss. I can't remember who took it into his office and placed it on his desk, but I do remember it was just before he stuck his head out of the office door and yelled, "Neffy, get your fucking ass into my office right now!"

Knowing now that my reputation had preceded me, and being in the process of stripping down for a much-needed shower, I pondered whether to slip on some pants before going into the office. Bill Zettlemoyer, known to the riggers as "Humphrey", looked at me and laughed, saying "Go in naked to see him."

Much too modest to do that, I wrapped a towel around me and shuffled into his office, wearing my wooden shower shoes. My appearance at his door in this state seemed to throw him off a bit and he laughed and said, "I was told you riggers were crazy!"

"Most of us are certifiable. But you hurt our feelings with that giant padlock," I lied.

What he seemed to understand pretty quickly was that we were much different from the guys who had worked for him previously. If he pushed, we pushed back. He laughed and tossed the padlock to me.

"Here's a souvenir for you!"

After that incident, a standard Bethlehem Steel padlock was installed, which almost everyone had a key for. That giant padlock still resides in a prominent place on the workbench in my basement.

29 THE BLASTING CREW

When a blast furnace goes cold, any molten iron which was below the tap hole on the furnace solidifies. This is called the "salamander". It is usually about four feet thick and covers the base of the furnace hearth. The only way to remove it is to lance holes into it, cool it down, pack it with explosives and blow it, fracturing it into several pieces like a jigsaw puzzle. A crane is needed to pull them out.

In the summer of 1984 we began a rebuild of the "B" blast furnace. This was the first in line of the furnaces which were still operational. "A" furnace, which is the smallest of the still-existing furnaces visible today, sits at the west end. It went dormant in 1960. After that it was mainly used by employees as an awesome perch for viewing the fireworks if you were unfortunate enough to get stuck working the Fourth of July or the last day of Musikfest.

At the onset of a furnace rebuild, everything in that furnace is stripped out of it, leaving a hollow steel shell. Tons of debris, bricks pipes, and hundreds of brick cooling devices are thrown onto piles for removal. When the furnace is finally cleaned of all debris, when you walk inside it resembles a hollow pineapple. Air movers are installed at various levels, aimed at a counter-clockwise angle to facilitate smoke removal while the workers are lancing holes in the solid iron.

I spent the entire third week of August 1984 as a rigger

lancer, working sixteen hour shifts. Brad Jones called us all together at 7 AM and said "If you give me nine holes per day, we'll cool them down, pack them and blow them, and you can be out of here by 9 PM."

We worked as teams, alternating duties. With the ambient temperature hovering around ninety degrees, it became an almost unbearable job. But the lure of working with high explosives kept us from dropping out. When it was my turn to lance, I suited up. It took about ten minutes to put on the assorted protective gear: fire retardant jacket and pants, shoe covers, welder's shield and gloves. You were then hoisted in a work cage attached to a block which came down from the top of the furnace. You started about twenty feet above the surface of solid iron, holding a thirty foot lancing rod. Your partner would walk over and light the end of your lance with an oxy/acetylene torch. The lances were about ¾" in diameter and were filled with magnesium wire. When the end was lit, you turned on a valve blowing oxygen through it. The resulting flame was about two thousand degrees and could cut through solid iron. You simply poked the end into the iron below, cutting a six inch diameter hole and washing the molten iron away.

This wasn't too bad while starting the hole, but when you were about three feet down, the molten iron had nowhere to go but straight up. While the lances got shorter the crane operator would lower you down closer to the hole. Even with all the protective gear, drops of molten iron would find their way through. Melting the iron also produces a noxious orange/brown smoke which required us to wear double canister respirators.

One of the most remarkable sights I ever saw was while suspended in that furnace. While changing to a new lancing rod, I flipped up my visor and was awe struck. The air movers used to remove the smoke from the furnace had created a vortex. I was in the center of a two hundred foot man-made tornado.

The job did take its toll. You would actually lose three to five pounds per shift, become borderline dehydrated, and suffer the pain of small molten iron burns. But this was endured for the chance to blow something up.

At about 4 PM each day we would have our nine holes finished and would begin cooling them down. Fire hoses were brought in and filled the holes. It would take them about an hour to cool off. On the first day Brad Jones, our boss and the only licensed blaster in the plant gave us our first lesson in explosives.

At the time we were using Tovex, a nitro based gel. Each unit weighed one pound and had a similar appearance to a liverwurst. The end was pierced with a brass rod and an electric blasting cap inserted in the hole. The wires were then wrapped around the unit with a half-hitch knot. Nine initial units were made, one for each hole. We were then instructed to place the primed charge in the bottom of each hole.

Now the order was to load five more sticks into each hole. This is about where the discipline broke down and the whole operation turned into a fucking Marx Brothers movie. I was loading Hole 3. To my left at Hole 2 I see Rigger Dick Medlecot throwing Tovex into the hole two at a time. I looked over at Dick and asked "How many did you put in?"

He looked over at me laughing and said "eight". About this time Brad came by, supervising the loading.

"Dick, how many do you have in the hole?" he asked.

Dick replied "Three".

"Put two more in and pack it with mud. Make sure the blast wires stick out of the hole at least three feet," Brad said.

"Okay boss," Dick said, and obediently added the charges, bringing Hole 2's load to ten. When all the holes were loaded we used the overhead crane to lower two foot thick rope blast mats over the holes. One rigger asked Brad if we should remove the four drop work lights we had hanging in the furnace suspended by one hundred foot cords.

"No," Brad said. "They'll be alright." As Brad wired all of the holes to a single line we all retreated to the cast floor shanty, about one hundred feet from the blast zone. The blast crew that day was Dick, myself, Les Clore, Charley Walp, Carl Rieker, Bob Schleicher, Barry Botts, Bob Solt, Tom OHaire, Bruce Ward, Carl Moyer, Foreman Ernie Smith and Howard "the Mudman" Bowers. A few minutes later, Brad comes in with a roll of wire attached to the blast holes. Brad waited until the plant patrol officers cleared the area of personnel for a distance of two hundred yards. A portable air whistle was activated with ten short blasts. Brad then wired the explosives to the blasting box. Three long blasts on the whistle mean the blast was imminent. Brad yelled "Fire in the hole", and slowly lifted the handle on the blasting box. Pushing it down would make the magneto inside generate enough voltage to set off the charges.

What happened next went down in the annals of rigger lore and has been told at every rigger reunion since. Accompanied by German music wafting across the river from Musikfest, Brad pushed down on the handle. As the resulting blast shook the entire furnace and knocked a few of us to the floor, the cast floor door opens and Carl Moyer falls into the room with ketchup poured on his head and running down his face. Foreman Ernie Smith and Brad went ballistic. When Carl got up laughing, everyone else burst out laughing with him. The mirth was short-lived. The plant patrol radioed to Brad that chunks of iron were landing in the Lehigh River.

I looked at Brad and said "What the fuck are they worried about? So we killed a few fish."

Looking back at me he said, "Hey Einstein. What makes you think it only went one way."

When the smoke cleared we saw that the rope mat over Hole 2 had disintegrated and two of the drop lights were wrapped around the superstructure two hundred feet above us. The other two were missing and never found. Two hours later we were informed that we had perforated several employee cars parked in a lot on Third Street.

We did better on the Tuesday and Wednesday shots, had a misfire on Thursday, and by Friday we were seasoned pros.

30 BLOWED UP

I don't suppose anyone really knows the exact date when the Rigger Department in the Bethlehem plant shifted its major endeavors from high steel construction and maintenance to demolition and coordinated destruction. It's inherent in most individuals to find great satisfaction in building things or finishing some task. On the opposite side of this coin is an utter fascination by most people in watching things being destroyed, which is most evident by the teeming crowds of onlookers at the location when crews are imploding some large building which has outlived its usefulness.

In the late 1980's the executives at Bethlehem Steel realized that if unused buildings within the vast area of the plant were razed, the amount of property taxes paid to the City of Bethlehem would be significantly reduced by hundreds of thousands of dollars. At the onset of this money-saving policy, it was determined that in-house employees would be used. And most of this work fell into the lap of our own Rigger Department.

Most of us in the Department had already spent one or two decades of our lives erecting buildings, rebuilding blast furnaces, and doing high area maintenance. One might think that tearing things down that you had spent a chunk of your life erecting and maintaining would be depressing or at least disturbing, but this was not the case. Being the mercenaries that we were, our paychecks were the ultimate aim. The bad boys of Bethlehem Steel took to the change quite easily. In fact, we took to knocking buildings down or blowing them up like ducks take to water.

One benefit in tearing buildings down is the chance to harvest items of a bit of value. On one job Rigger Al Lotti and I were dismantling large public address speakers mounted high up on the walls. Taking apart the speakers revealed a large magnet capable of lifting fifty pounds. We would pass them out to other employees who were fishermen. The magnets worked remarkably well for retrieving keys or fishing gear that fell overboard.

While dismantling a few speakers in a building scheduled for demolition, a foreman from another department saw us and reported the incident to our boss Brad Jones. He called us in at the end of the day. I was standing next to Al waiting for the interrogation to begin when the door opened and Brad came in.

"Why the fuck are you guys stealing magnets from those speakers?" he asked.

As I was about to plead ignorance to these false charges, the magnet I had secreted in my coat pocket decided to attach itself to the filing cabinet that I was standing next to with a loud, audible "clunk". Looking over at Al, we both only smiled, trying to retain our dignity.

Brad looked sternly at us and said, "God damn it, I want an answer."

Without smiling, Al looked at Brad and said, "We take the magnets home and bury them in our backyards so UFO's can't land there."

Not knowing whether to scream or laugh at us, Brad opted for laughing. Pointing to the door, he said "You two fucking nuts get out of my fucking office!"

I smiled, thinking "Like I never heard that before."

When we had begun our scorched earth campaign, buildings had been dropping like dominoes. Then we came to the gas engine house, adjacent to the A Blast Furnace at the west end of the blast furnace line.

It was a forty-foot high steel frame and brick building housing six rather large gas engines. We had already begun working to dismantle the first engine. We had spent the previous ten days dismantling the sixty-ton flywheel which was attached to its side. It was taken apart by using eight-foot long oxyacetylene burning torches. Each wheel was removed in approximately five to seven ton blocks of steel, hoisted by the building's twenty-five ton capacity overhead crane, which was operated by a rigger. The powerhouse crane operators had deemed us too crazy and dangerous to work with. I suppose there was merit in their assessment of our work practices.

After loading a fishtail dump truck which had a load capacity of twenty-five tons, we watched it going down the road on its run to the scrap yard with its tires looking like water balloons. The driver came back an hour later spitting fire.

"You fuckin assholes overloaded my truck!" he screamed. He became even more irate with six riggers smiling insipidly back at him.

"What was the weight at the truck scale?" I asked.

"Why the fuck do you want to know that?"

"Well, we had a pool going after you left. We all kicked in one dollar to guess the load weight."

"43 tons," he answered.

Looking at the sheet, I yelled "With a guess of 42 tons, Charley Walp wins!"

"You fuckin guys are nuts," the driver said as he turned and walked away.

"Hey driver," a rigger yelled, holding up his eight-foot torch. "Try driving this fire stick for ninety minutes straight in all those sparks and smoke."

That seemed to soften the driver's sour mood so to placate him we sent him out with a twenty ton load on his next run. He left smiling.

After cutting off everything on the engine that we could, we set up to cut into the actual engine itself. Without plans it was a slow process. We worked in teams of two burners. One would suit up in a fire retardant suit, gloves, and head gear with a dark lens covered by steel mesh. Since visibility was limited, the other burner on the team would assist by lighting the end of the eight-foot torch.

We were about three hours into our 4 PM to 12 AM middle shift. I had just finished my one-hour tour of attempting to cut through into the engine housing. After unsuiting, and handing the gear to my partner Tony "Draz" Drazenovich, I laid down on a bench, soaked and exhausted, and lit up a cigarette. It took Tony about ten minutes to suit up and adjust the pressure on the tanks which fed his cutting torch. We would burn pieces out of the engine housing for the next hour, taking us up to lunchtime. He nodded to me that he was ready to start, and I got up and walked over to him. As he turned on the valves of his torch, I held up the end of his torch and lit it with my spark lighter. As he started cutting into the housing, I noticed the smoke coming off of the molten flow wasn't rising to the building ceiling, but was being sucked back into the engine.

About this time, Tony had a flameout. This happens when the torch operator gets the tip too close to what he is attempting to cut. Tony left the torch tip, which was still pushing out gas and oxygen, on the edge of the piece he was cutting. I walked over to him to relight his torch. I lifted up the end of it, and instead of using my spark lighter I blew on the top of my cigarette and held it to his torch. It lit and as I walked past Tony, he motioned a thank you wave.

That was about two seconds before the explosion. The concussion from the blast hurled Tony and me about eight feet from where we had been standing. I was lying face down in the dirt and Tony was lying on his back about five feet away from me. Between us was a ten pound chunk of the housing. All I could remember was the sensation of being punched by a giant invisible fist.

I did a quick evaluation of my predicament. I was aware of my situation, which was good. My arms and legs were still working, also good. As I looked over to Draz, he rolled over and got up onto his hands and knees. His large fire retardant head gear had been blown off. His head slowly turns and as he looks up at me, he says "You know, I have a noise restriction." Everyone there started laughing. We knew Draz was healthy, albeit somewhat sore and shaken.

The resulting investigation explained what had happened. Draz had burned a hole into the piston shaft, a cylindrical chamber about two feet in diameter and twelve feet long. When the engine had been shut down, the giant piston had stopped midway in the shaft. When Draz's torch flamed out, the gas still emanating from it flowed into the piston shaft, creating a highly explosive mixture. After his torch was relit, touching it to the hole "lit the fuse".

It was a tough lesson learned, but we now knew how to dismantle the others safely.

One of these engines has been saved for its historic value. It is located east of the Levitt Pavillion at Steel Stax. Every time I pass by it walking to a concert, I am reminded of the night one of its five brethren decided to strike back against its ultimate demise.

31 SAVING THE HOT END

Beginning in the mid to late 1980's, there were doubts about how long the flagship plant of the Bethlehem Steel Corporation, situated in Bethlehem, PA, would endure. The plant, constructed in the late nineteenth and early twentieth centuries, was entirely reliant on railroads. I remember a trip to the South Side shopping district with my father to buy my baseball shoes for my first year in Little League. Stopped by a passing coal train, we sat in our Ford for at least thirty minutes. Sensing my impatience, my father said, "Relax, that train means I have a job and extra money to buy those shoes." The logic of that was lost on my nine-year-old mind that day, and within twenty minutes I was sitting on a bench in Marcus Sporting Goods trying on my new baseball spikes. A mere twenty years later I finally realized what my father meant.

Steel mills built by Bethlehem Steel in subsequent years were constructed with knowledge of the failings and deficiencies of the initial mill. The Burns Harbor IN and Sparrows Point MD steel mills were newer and much more logistically suited for manufacturing steel. Both plants were situated on large waterways and products needed were brought in by ore freighter, eliminating many of the handling procedures at the local plant, and making these plants much more efficient.

The "Hot End" at the Bethlehem plant referred to any department which was directly involved in the steelmaking process.

The method for producing steel is extensive and complicated. It began in the coal fields of the Coke Oven Division, where coal was heated and compressed to form coke, necessary for the production of iron. Vast yards holding thousands of tons of other ores required to make iron were moved by gigantic ore bridges onto conveyer lines to the treatment facilities of the Sintering Plant. Fuel for the blast furnaces, highly flammable coke oven gas, was piped through a series of 36" pipes which ran for miles and zigzagged through the plant from its source in the ovens of the Coke Plant.

The movement of these essential products ran on an elaborate schedule of trains and trucks which had to be strictly adhered to in order to keep the blast furnaces operational. In its heyday, the local plant had up to seven blast furnaces producing iron at any given time. Access to this line of furnaces was provided by narrow gauge and broad gauge rail lines running atop the elevated Hoover/Mason trestle. After working repair shifts at the Sintering Plant, riggers working out of the Lehigh Rigger building would frequently hop aboard ore cars moving down the tracks to the blast furnaces. Nicknamed the "Hooterville Trolley" by Rigger Steve Gombosi, it was a welcome switch to a long walk back to our shop hauling our tools and gear.

Any deviation in bringing ore and coke to the furnaces could result in a shutdown. An operating or "hot" furnace could be shut down for repairs for a maximum of thirty hours in a procedure called "banking". After this time the furnace would cool to a degree where bringing it back online would not be possible. The iron would solidify in the furnace, fifty feet or more higher than the tap hole, turning the entire structure into one solid unusable mass.

Iron created in the blast furnace is vital in the production of steel. The iron was tapped from the furnace and separated from slag, then funneled down brick-lined troughs on the cast floor, where it spilled into "submarine" railroad cars. These cars would transfer the iron to the Basic Oxygen Furnace located in the Saucon Division.

After being loaded, the subs, weighing in excess of three hundred tons, were moved over a small iron bridge which incorporated a weighing scale at its far end with only one track onto and off of the scale. This created a serious bottleneck. The system worked smoothly for many years, until one very hot summer's day.

A sub being pushed onto the scale by a PBNE engine collapsed through the bridge and buried itself into the soft earth to a depth of about six feet. It was close to noon when the alarm went out calling for riggers and carpenters to report to the area.

When we arrived at the site, it looked as though a bomb had gone off. The small bridge and rails were bent and twisted. The rail carriages on which the sub had travelled had detached and the sub was buried halfway into the ground. You could feel the heat emanating from the sub at fifty feet. To my right, the carpenter service truck was being unloaded. Carpenter Tim Brown, wrapping cables around 12 x 12 blocking timbers, looked over at us. Pointing at the sub, he smiled and said, "After this job, you're balls will be hanging down to your ankles, fellas!"

We all laughed, then groaned, visualizing the picture he had just planted in our heads. While Jeff Gehringer and Bruce Ward were using cutting torches to remove the twisted steel, our service truck arrived with two massive lifting cables. They were braided steel, each twenty feet long with an eight inch diameter, weighing in at fifteen hundred pounds. Smaller cables, shackles, shovels and other gear were unloaded and a forklift was used to move the gear as close to the sub as it could safely do.

The basic job wasn't too complicated but was extremely dangerous. Carpenters would first move in to secure the sub by blocking it up to prevent it from shifting. Riggers would go in next, tunneling under the car, to get the lifting cables around it. Finally, after hoisting the car into the air, riggers, along with a track gang crew would work under the hanging three hundred ton monster to replace the bridge and rails.

At the onset of the job, we were advised by blast furnace supervision that the furnace was banked and we had 24 hours to complete the job. With this the only operational furnace, going cold meant the decision would be made to close down the Hot End, leading to the loss of hundreds of jobs for our union brothers and sisters.

After the news circulated, many foremen from throughout the plant showed up in their green hard hats, creating, as Rigger Bob Schleicher so eloquently put it, a cabbage patch. This would always happen on large or unique jobs, but this time it was quite different.

Their jobs were directly tied to the outcome as well.

Our job began when the car was blocked and secured. The east end of the car was relatively clear, so debris was removed and one of the huge lifting cables was snaked under it. On the west end of the sub two rigger gangs, totaling eight men, began tunneling under it from either end. The gang I worked in included Dennis Hoffman, Al Lotti, and Willy D. Chain. Digging like frantic moles from the opposite side were Tom OHaire, Fritz Werner, Joe Cheszar and John Weiss. After about ten minutes most of us stripped to the waist, shedding hard hats, safety glasses, shirts and gloves. A fire hose was set up and after about five minutes of digging we would emerge from the hole and get hosed off like circus animals. It took us about ninety minutes of constant digging to cut through. Using a five ton air hoist which was mounted to a building column, we drug the lifting cable through.

While we were taking a well-deserved break the enormous mobile lifting cranes crawled slowly toward us. Pulling onto the job site, the operators jumped off their rigs and came over to see where wanted to spot them. The cranes were manufactured by Krupp Industries of Germany. In size and lifting capacity the rigs were awesome. Looking over them took me fondly back to the days when I would spend endless hours playing with my older brothers' Erector Set while they were in school.

After drooling over the rigs, most of us were snapped out of our reverie by the urgency of the task at hand, and the growing anxiety of our ever-expanding audience which now included a few Italian designer silk suits from the fourteenth floor.

A mobile crane's greatest lifting capacity is a short boom in an almost vertical position, set up as close as you can get to the object you are lifting. We spent two hours working the rigs in close to the sub. Light was fading, so portable high intensity lamps were set up making the whole area look like a monster truck rally on a West Virginia Friday night. Thirty minutes later the sub was cradled by the two heavy lifting cables and the rigs were ready to make the lift. The signal was given and the sub rose from its hole. The cranes never uttered a groan, lifting and holding a load in excess of three hundred tons.

Exhausted, we moved in under the load and rigged up new

heavy span beams and railroad rails to set the sub onto. This was the most frightening part of the entire job. Positioned under the load, we used poles to spin the sub and line up the wheels on the rails. When it landed safely onto the rails I looked at my watch. It was 12:15 AM! We had beaten the 24 hour deadline and completed the job in twelve!

The molten iron in the sub car would solidify, making it a dead loss. But the track bottleneck had been cleared and other cars could resume feeding the needs of the furnaces. The problem car ended up abandoned on a side track near E furnace where it stood for many years.

After unhooking the cables, moving the cranes off sight and cleaning up the job site we shouldered our tool belts and slowly headed off, thinking of how good that shower was going to feel. As we were leaving, a Seville Road suit was standing there shaking our hands as we passed by, thanking us.

We saved the "Hot End" that day, and it would go on producing steel for an additional seven years. That is not, however, what drove us. As riggers, we worked many dangerous jobs. It was the spirit of competitiveness and the belief that we were the toughest and possibly the craziest group of workers that Bethlehem Steel had ever produced. We knew how to survive. The question now was: how long would our steel mill survive?

32 THE HIGH HOUSE

It is a common belief in the world of the paranormal that sudden, unexpected and violent death creates inexplicable phenomena.

Early in my career as a rigger, I was working a night shift in the Coke Oven Division coal fields. It was a hot August night, and I was walking in from the parking lot at the beginning of the shift with Rigger Don Boose. He stopped to light up a cigarette. Looking at me, he pointed toward the coke ovens, pushing product out into a receiving car, and glowing a bright orange in the night sky.

"Neffy, doesn't it look like we're walking through the gates of Hell?"

"It feels like it," I said.

We changed into our work clothes and headed over to our job. That night we would be repairing the car tip, a large machine which would clamp entire railroad gondola cars down, then roll them over to empty the contents. The welding machine we would be using that night was situated in a deep pit at the bottom of a flight of stairs, sixty feet below us.

One of my jobs that night was adjusting the welding machine as per orders from the rigger welder. At the beginning of our shift, I descended the staircase with a two-way radio and a flashlight. I threw the toggle switch to turn on the welding machine, and waited for the welder to call me.

To understand what happened next, I must explain how this

welding machine functioned. Using it created an immense amount of heat. If the machine started to overheat, it was designed to turn itself off, preventing a possible meltdown. It was well capable of shutting itself off, but it required a human hand to flip the stiff toggle switch on.

The welder called me on the radio and I adjusted the amperage. It took about three adjustments until he was satisfied. During the ten minutes I was in the pit, I had an eerie feeling that I was not alone. Perhaps it was knowing that several employees had lost their lives in that particular area over the years. I shined my flashlight around the area, reaffirming that I was alone, and began to ascend the stairway. When I reached the top the welder motioned to me, pointing at his welding handle and shaking his head back and forth, meaning he had no power.

Leaning over the pit railing I heard nothing but silence, meaning the welding machine had shut down. Heading back down the stairway, the clanking of my tool belt seemed to bolster my lagging courage. I suppose I assumed that the noise would frighten any unseen specter away.

I walked over to the machine and switched it on. As I turned and started up the stairs I heard an audible click and thought that the welding machine, being a rather old one, had seen its last days and would have to be mercifully put down. As I walked back over to it, shining my flashlight on the on/off switch, an unseen hand pushed the switch to the "On" position.

I really don't remember my feet touching any of the steps until I was halfway up the staircase. Seeing the look on my face when I emerged, my fellow riggers began laughing.

"I see you have met the ghost in the pit," Donny said.

"Yeah," I replied. "And you can go fuck yourself if you think I'm going down there again!"

"It's happened before," Don said. "Just something playing tricks on us.

If sudden death can cause paranormal anomalies, the Bethlehem Steel plant's "High House" would rate high on the light for being haunted. It was also the site for my last close encounter with the grim reaper during my days as a rigger.

The "High House" is still visible today, situated about

halfway across the span of the Minsi Trail Bridge. Bethlehem residents usually refer to it as the High House, but it was known to employees as the Number 3 Treatment Facility. It was erected in the early twentieth century as a facility for heat treating or annealing rather large gun barrels. The building housed two large vertical furnaces which extended forty feet below ground level. It also had a large vertical annealing tank, a vertical assembly pit, and a rather unique one hundred ton chain-operated overhead crane which had no electric motors and was entirely operated by hand.

Its true claim to fame, however, was more sinister. This was the building where the worst accident in the history of the Bethlehem Steel plant happened, claiming eight workers' lives. In October of 1945 two workers were overcome by gas from the furnace. Six other employees perished trying to rescue them.

When I started my career at Beth Steel, operations at the Number 3 Treatment building had already been shut down. Our warehouse building where the Rigger Department stored most of its heavy equipment was adjacent to the High House.

The unique crane in #3 Treatment had come under the scrutiny of the Smithsonian Institution, which was intending to possibly harvest it as a relic of the Industrial Revolution. Plans to remove it for placement in a museum had begun. A photography team arrived from Washington DC to photograph the crane from various angles. They met with an operator from the Trucking Department whose high reach bucket truck would allow them to get up to the level of the crane for their photo shoot.

They had only been working for a few minutes when the lifting rig unexpectedly malfunctioned. Unable to go up or down, the operator only had lateral control. This he used to position the bucket five feet away from a stairway landing about sixty feet above the floor.

Rigger foreman Butch Horn called me on the radio and asked me to bring two eight foot safety planks, climbing harnesses, and ropes. Carrying all that gear up the staircase to the level of the stranded photo crew, we spanned the planks from the bucket to the stairway, then walked across to give the photo crew their safety harnesses. After adjusting their harnesses and tying a long safety rope to each of them, I climbed higher up the staircase to rig a safety line. I was unable to coax the crew to walk across the planks, and they opted to crawl across on their hands and knees instead. Upset by the experience, the photographer still managed to take a few pictures of his rescuers, and promised to send copies to us. If he ever did, I never received one. The strangest thing about the incident was, as soon as the photo crew left, the bucket truck started up and ran flawlessly.

A few years after this incident, I had the last near-death encounter of my career, which had nothing to do with the paranormal and everything to do with human error. During the late 1980's I decided to take better care of my health. The company had opened a fitness center that the plant employees could use, so I took full advantage of it. After a slight bout with pneumonia, I took the opportunity to quit smoking. The rising cost of cigarettes also helped me quit. I am not referring to the rising retail cost of cigarettes, but to the rising cost my co-workers would charge me.

I never smoked outside of the workplace. And I realized quite early in my smoking career that if I carried a pack of cigarettes, I would smoke the entire pack during my eight hour shift. To limit my cigarette use I would purchase single cigarettes from my rigger pals. I believe it started about ten cents per smoke. Due to spiraling inflation, the price slowly rose to twenty-five cents. Then fifty cents, where it held for quite some time until Rigger Dennis Hoffman began charging the outrageous sum of one dollar a piece. To Dennis' credit, I must say, he did smoke Marlboros, not those dried out skunk piss generics that everyone was buying. Thinking of the money that I would save by quitting, in retrospect by jacking up the price he actually aided me in kicking the habit. And for that, I thank him.

As part of my fitness regime I also began walking to work. From Darto's, a wonderful little restaurant on North St. in Bethlehem, it is about 2 ½ miles to the plant. After having breakfast, I would either walk or bike to work.

One beautiful October day, while walking to work across the Minsi Trail Bridge, I noticed that the thirty foot mast rising from the roof of the High House had been hit by lightning in the previous night's storm. About four feet above the roof the pipe was bent at a thirty degree angle, leaning east toward the bridge. Anyone could see that if the pipe should break free and slide down the roof, it would be launched onto the bridge, possibly harpooning a passing vehicle.

As a Bethlehem Steel employee, you were drilled constantly on safe work practices and recognizing unsafe situations in the plant. As a rigger you also periodically went out on a building inspection gang. This was a crew that inspected anything in the plant for its structural integrity.

When I went to work that morning, I dutifully informed the proper authorities of the Number Three Treatment broken mast, which I found out was, in reality, a lightning arrestor. It had nobly performed its job that past evening, but had succumbed to the ravages of wind and weather, and the only option left was to remove it. My report was filed in October and it wasn't until the following April that it was scheduled to be removed.

I was informed that I was to be the burner in the aerial gang on this job. My job would be to burn a hole in the pipe, insert a cable through it, and attach it to a chain hoist hanging on the crane hook. A crew on the building's roof would then cut it free from its base. At the onset, a crane with high reach capabilities would be positioned in the southbound lane of the bridge, closed to traffic by the Bethlehem police.

Ideally, two cranes should have been used: one to hold the aerial crew in a work basket; and one crane to handle the mast that was being removed. Frugality had triumphed over safety, however, and only one crane was going to be used. I realized this when we were loading our gear into the basket. I had loaded my burning tanks, hose, torch, and cables. My partner, Rigger Nick Pidstawski, came over carrying a chain hoist capable of lifting five tons. He hung it on the same crane hook that our basket was attached to.

"You mean the same crane is going to hold us and the load?" I asked.

"It has to. We only have the one crane at our disposal," Nick said.

Pete Chando and Al Lotti were already on the roof, ready to cut the mast free, when the crane began lifting us up two hundred feet to our job. When we reached our position, I looked down at the crane on the bridge. It was blocked out and stabilized the proper way. But from our position it looked frighteningly like a Match Box toy.

Trying not to think of the dreadful history of the building we were suspended over, I lowered my burning goggles, lit my torch, and started to cut a hole through the pipe. As I started to cut through, though, I noticed the mast was made of X pipe. This is a pipe with very thick walls, weighing much more than a standard pipe.

In the twenty years since this incident, I have toned down my opinion of the job planner to a mere fucking moron. When he planned the job he never took into consideration that it might be a heavier pipe. In a very few minutes we were going to be a two hundred pound tuna hanging on a five pound test line.

We ran a cable through the hole and attached it to the chain hoist hanging from the block. Nick gave the signal over the radio for the crew on the roof to cut the mast. This is where the job went horribly wrong.

As the mast swung free, we bobbed up and down for a few seconds, and then came the last thing we ever wanted to hear. Walter Holtzhafer, our foreman who was keeping watch on the crane, yelled over the radio "The crane is tipping!"

It is always said that in moments when one thinks one is going to die, your entire life passes before your eyes. Hanging like a trout, two hundred feet up on a tipping crane, all I could think of was "what a stupid fucking way to die."

I have seen cranes tip over, and usually the first thing that happens is the operator jumps free of the rig. This crane operator did not leave his cab, and that's what saved our lives. He stayed with his tipping crane, carefully moved his boom up, brought the center of gravity back over his rig, and lowered us to the ground. He risked serious injury or possibly his life to stay with us. This was one thing I always liked about the job I had chosen. Some union brother or sister always had your back.

I survived the last few years the plant was open with hardly a scratch, much to the amazement of my guardian angel.

33 EPILOG

After the Hot End shut down in the mid-nineties, the Bethlehem plant became a hollow shell of its former self. Employees were reduced from thousands to hundreds. The only operational departments left were a few machine shops and the Coke Oven Division.

I always thought that I would retire before the end came for the plant. We went out together.

The last weeks before the end came were mostly an anti-climax. Since the layoffs of workers in the mid-eighties, there had been rumors almost daily that the plant was closing. The end caused scarcely a ripple of emotion for most workers. It was like a ship slipping beneath the waves.

It was the friendships with coworkers that had the most impact. After shaking hands and saying goodbye, I slipped off my tool belt, put it in my toolbox, and never looked back.

Whenever I pass the Steel stacks and furnaces, I begin to reminisce, not of cold steel but of the friendship of my union brothers and sisters whom I had the pleasure to work with all those many years.

As I was sitting at Levitt Pavillion one evening watching one of their wonderful shows, I remembered an incident that happened during the first week I was a rigger. Walking under "B" blast furnace with Billy Arnold, a longtime rigger, I heard a loud bang like a gunshot.

"Billy, what the hell was that?"

He turned to me and said "A rivet let go." He explained that most of the structures in the plant were built when riveting was common. If the riveted steel isn't painted, water seeps into the joints, and becomes rust which has the potential to expand and pop the rivets.

"That's why Bethlehem Steel paints the furnaces every five years," he said.

The furnaces and stacks haven't been painted in over twenty years. Maybe the colored lights are the only thing that's holding them together. The Company failed, but the furnaces and I are still standing.

ABOUT THE AUTHOR

Larry Neff was born and raised in Bethlehem, PA, the son of a steelworker. He worked at Bethlehem Steel from 1972 until the plant closed in 1999. His love of climbing helped him earn a place with the rigger crews that did the jobs deemed too high, too hard, or too dangerous for other Bethlehem Steel departments to handle. Larry has two sons, Jared, 33, and Adam, 29. He still lives in Bethlehem, still loves hiking and climbing, and is working on his next book.

Made in the USA
Charleston, SC
24 October 2014